Lalitha Indranee Brodie
E-mail: lalitha.brodie7@hotmail.com
Bi-lingual Blog: www.lalithabrodie.weebly.com
Tel: 905-270-1214 / 416-907-6897

PEACE WITH JUSTICE
BY
LALITHA BRODIE

Published By
AHILAN ASSOCIATES
TORONTO CANADA 2005

ISBN No.   0-9685364-2-5

I DEDICATE THIS BOOK
PEACE WITH JUSTICE
WITH LOVE AND GRATITUDE
TO MY PARENTS

V.A.NADARAJAH (Supdt.of Audits)
30.4.1907 - 3.5.1971

NALLAMMAH (SARAS) NADARAJAH
5.5.1913 - 12.2.2002
AND MY GRANDMOTHER

SINNAMMAH NAGALINGAM
1893 – 1983

1

PEACE WITH JUSTICE

By

LALITHA BRODIE

115 Conley Street
Vaughn, Ontario L4J 2X4
Canada

E-mail: lalitha.brodie022@sympatico.ca

First Edition - 2005

Lalitha Brodie's Photographs by Irene Borins Ash
www.ireneborinsash.com

Published By:
AHILAN ASSOCIATES
Toronto Canada 2005
E-mail: ahilanassociates@sympatico.ca

ISBN: 0-9685364-2-5

FOREWORD

It is with immense pleasure and pride that I write this foreword for Mrs.Lalitha Brodie's book of poems, Peace with Justice. I have been an admirer of her multifaceted activities for over three decades both in Jaffna, Sri Lanka and here in Canada, which prompted us at Tamils' Information to grant her the gold medal and award for Social Services in the year 2000.

Mrs.Lalitha Brodie, well recognized amongst our South Asian Tamil community and the Canadian mainstream, is a devoted wife, mother, grandmother, TV/Radio Producer/Broadcaster, cook, counselor, artist and poet/ writer in both English and Tamil languages. She is a caring social worker who has dedicated her life to volunteer service. It is significant that with her excellent command of both Tamil and English languages, she is the first woman from our community to publish a book of poems in English, dispelling the myth that we are not proficient in English.

It is great that Peace with Justice proclaims not only her varied thoughts and feelings, but also effectively disseminates the story and struggle of our people in Tamil Eelam to the rest of the world. Her vivid words also record the history of her time, for the benefit of future generations. May her prophetic vision of the Dawn of Thamil Eelam in her final poem in section 2, materialize soon. May her amazing creativity continue.

Thiru S.Thiruchelvam
Veteran Journalist & Editor,
Tamils' Information Canada
E-mail: tamilsinfo@sympatico.ca

4

TABLE OF CONTENTS

8

INTRODUCTION

Lalitha Brodie and I have been colleagues for some

years in the Older Women's
Network, and I have watched
her grow as a poet in both depth
and dexterity. *Peace with
Justice* traces Lalitha's life in Sri
Lanka and that of her family, their
move to Canada, and their

reactions on a personal family level. Her poems also
embrace wider horizons from her perspective as a
deeply spiritual and philosophical woman who seeks
ardently to broaden her knowledge according to the
values she holds dear, those of "Love, Truth, Right
Conduct, Non-Violence, and Peace".

Her poems give us a vivid picture of the strife and
violence that have torn her native land and its divided
peoples. In prose poetry, we share with her not only
the tribulations of Sri Lanka, but also year by year the
violence that occurs across the world. Woven within
this broader tapestry is Lalitha's story, and that of her
family, immigrants who have pride in and love for
Canada, their adopted land.

UNITY IN DIVERSITY

*Traveling the Toronto TTC with passengers of a
multicultural flare
I daily marvel at the well-synchronized harmony
evident everywhere . . .*

PEACE AND HOPE

*We Tamils, hail from a war ravaged land
Tamil Eelam, crowning the North
And embracing the East
Of the emerald isle that is Sri Lanka.
Is it wrong for us to envisage freedom?
And long for an independent state of our own?*

These poems speak to us all, Tamils and others, verses
to touch the heart, enrich our knowledge of their
homeland and history, and to add another layer to
Canada's mosaic.

Ann Farrell

Ann Farrell, 80, has been a writer for much of her life,
starting in 1941 in the London office of the *Calcutta
Statesman* as a trainee reporter. After serving as a
radar operator during World War II, she worked as

10

a reporter in England and Germany before immigrating to Canada in 1949.

In Canada, she worked as reporter and editor in British Columbia, Ontario, and New Brunswick, with nine years on the *Toronto Star*. She has published (Fitzhenry & Whiteside) a biography of the CCF/NDP federal politician Grace MacInnis, and her memoirs with a New Brunswick publisher -contact peace2you@hotmail.com for details. Her poems have appeared in several editions of the National Library of Poetry. Mother of five children and grandmother to six, along with several other positions, Ann Farrell has been chair of the Older Women's Network and of the board of the OWN Co-op where she lives in downtown Toronto.

PREFACE

"A Bhaktha poet with a political conscience!" This is the thought that passed through my mind as I read the moving poems of Mrs.Lalitha Brodie. There is a clear note of love and reverence for the spiritual in these poems. There is also a strong moral perspective on life. I was reminded of female Bhakthi poets like Madhaviakka. While we have read the Bhakthi poets of the past in the translation of someone like the late scholar A.K.Ramanujan, in this collection we have the advantage of entering the world of Saivite religious sensibility directly in English, thanks to the skill of Mrs.Brodie.

However, the world of Mrs.Brodie is more complex. She is also aware of the geopolitical realities that have brought her to Canada as a refugee. This political sensibility and the desire for justice make her different from the Bhakthi poets of the past ages. Mrs.Brodie is clearly rooted in the modern social milieu-characterized by technology, urban life, ethnic conflict, cultural mixing and geographical tensions. Therefore, she can say "I bow my head" to Canada in one poem

12

and "I bow my head" to Sai Baba in another! This multiculturalism in the collection is interesting. In one poem, she is in an Indian Ashram as a devotee of Sai Baba; in another, she is enjoying the technology and comforts of Canada. Mrs.Brodie straddles both worlds-East and the West-comfortably. This ability to appreciate diverse experiences and cultures should be instructive for other Tamil immigrants. Too often, we adopt the new culture uncritically or retreat into our past blindly shuttling between two extremes. Mrs.Brodie is able to preserve the tension between cultures and respond to both of them.

These poems are also valuable as a stream of consciousness of an immigrant Tamil person. They open a window into the mind of a Tamil who has had to leave the traditional homeland for a new location. For people in such situations of exile, it is very important to write. Writing gives them ways of externalising their complex feelings and developing modes of adaptation to new experience. Though we have many young people from the community writing creatively these days, it is important to hear the voices of the older generation.

The latter belong to a neglected social group in Tamil Diaspora life. These poems enable us to understand the world of the older generation of Tamils who live in the West.

What we get from the mind of this senior citizen is a valuable moral sensibility. The seniors in our community have the moral authority to advice us on all matters of life. So, when Mrs.Brodie contemplates a recent case of divorce and reflects on the lesson (in poem 33), she easily fits into the role of an elder. Coming from a person of her status, the moralistic tone suits her poems and we accept her advice wholeheartedly. Furthermore, though the suffering of her people in the Tamil homeland pains her, she is never hateful of the perpetrators of this evil! She moves beyond hate and anger, to promote morals that lead to peace, love, and tolerance. We all need this attitude in a world that is increasingly torn by conflicts and warfare.

Professor A.Suresh Canagarajah
Department of English, Box B7-240
Baruch College
University of New York

INAUGURATION

It is a privilege and pleasure that our beloved president Mrs.Lalitha Brodie's book of poems 'Peace with Justice' is being launched today at this celebration of the third anniversary of Universal Community Help. Mrs. Brodie is our mother full of wisdom, who has supported us through thick and thin with her expertise and I just cannot find words enough to express how grateful I am to her.

Universal Community Help, our Non-profit organization, started on a small scale in 2002, as a sister organization to Thiruchchenthoor Murugan Hindu Temple, at #10-2400 Finch Ave.West serving our rapidly expanding South Asian Tamil community, numbering well over 300 000 in 2005. I am proud to record that UCH has grown rapidly and we are elated that our service Helping The Helpless, is creating history today.

It is Mrs.Lalitha Brodie's passion, commitment and experience as a psychological counsellor that created this interest in me, which prompted UCH to offer support-counselling services to the needy at Thiruchchenthoor Murugan Temple for the first time ever, in any Hindu temple in Canada. We were also the first, to successfully train and certify 12 Support Counselors by veteran Counselor Trainer Mrs.Indranee Abeyesekera in the summer of 2004. This experience has encouraged me to widen my knowledge and skills and after completing the Tamil Saiva Spiritual Support Certification Course recently, I am following more and more courses in the Mental Health field now.

The Tsunami disaster of 26.12.2004, where over 35 000 perished in our motherland Sri Lanka, makes us realize the urgent need, for psychological counseling services to the bereaved relatives there and here in Canada too. We envision training more counselors to serve here in Ontario and to visit Sri Lanka in rotation. We have great plans to widen our services to reach out to our Children, Youth, Families, Widows, Seniors, The Handicapped and focus more on Prevention of Disease, Abuse, Violence and Crime. May God Almighty bless our gifted guide Mrs.Lalitha Brodie with good health and longevity.

Gowrie Malan B Comm.Hons, Ehv.Can.
Founder/President Thiruchenthoor Murugan Hindu Temple Toronto, Founder/Director Universal Community Help Minister of Religion/Registrar of Marriages Ontario

PRELUDE

 My husband Rajah Brodie and I arrived in snow clad Canada as landed immigrants in February 1992, to join two sons domiciled here. The entirely new climate and lifestyle of the Tamil community in affluent Toronto, was so very different to all the challenges we had coped with in our Motherland, war ravaged Jaffna, Sri Lanka   Wide-eyed with wonder with the advanced technology of the west, we settled down to slowly start our integration into the Canadian Mainstream.

Rajah, who had worked as the superintendent on tea and rubber estates, including the largest tea estate in Sri Lanka Demodera Group (3200 acres), managed to find work in Toronto only as a security guard! I had to try very hard to expand my horizons in various ways, as I had absolutely no work experience. The rewards of diverse volunteerism as a psychological counselor and president of Mother's Front Chundikuli, Jaffna, helped me to enroll in 1992 as the first Asian volunteer at The Humber River Regional Hospital, Finch Site Toronto. I served as the Hon. Assistant Secretary for the St.Johns' Chundikuli Past Pupil's Association in 1993. M.P.Konesh, the globally recognized Tamil Composer-Musician-TV/Radio Broadcaster invited me

17

in 1994, into Radio Asia (Now ITR-International Tamil TV & Radio- www.tamil.fm - Please click archives to listen to my program 'Valarchi' on Thursdays 5 pm-6.20pm Canada Time). I gradually picked up my skills and am now competent in Program Production, Broadcasting and Telecasting as well as computer literacy.

As a seeker on the spiritual path, I am a Sathiya Sai Baba devotee from 1972 and have visited Puttaparthi, India eight times (www.sathyasai). I am a member from 1992 of Sukyo Mahikari, a Global Spiritual Organization from Japan. Daily meditation from 1983 has helped me to pave my own unique path with help from several spiritual leaders like Maharaji www.maharaji.net, Sri Vasudeva of Trinidad - www.blue_star.tstt.net and Yogi Satyam, who initiated me into Kriya Yoga in Toronto in 2002 www.kriyayoga_yogisatyam.org . I was on retreat at Yogi Satyam's Ashram at Sangam, Jhunsi, Allahabad, India, during the Magha Mela Festival, January to March 2004. I am most grateful to The Creative Writing Groups of The Toronto Senior Tamil Center and OWN - The Ontario Older Women's Network, (info@olderwomen'snetwork.org) Toronto, for encouraging and publishing some of my earlier poems. I trust that this book will inspire other women to join our fold and reap the rewards of all OWN activities, along with wings for their words. I also wish to thank

Thiru Thiruchelvam, Ann Farrell, Professor Suresh Canagarajah and Gowri Malan for their contributions - I must mention that this collection includes several poems written after I received their contributions. I plan to share the profits from the sale of this book to benefit Shanthiyaham, The Psychological Counseling Center at No.15 Kachcheri Nallur Road, Jaffna, Sri Lanka.

I do feel sorry that I did not start writing earlier, but it is better late than never! It is indeed rewarding that I am now a well-recognised Broadcaster/Telecaster and write extensively in both English and Tamil. My continuing Tamil articles from April 2003 titled Prayers For Personal Growth, adapted mainly from Iyanla Vanzant's book 'Until Today', in bi-monthly Vlambaram, seem to touch the lives of many Tamils, and bring me a lot of telephone calls (www.vlambaram.com). I am glad that Malan and Gowri, Founder Directors of Thiruchchenthoor Murugan Hindu Temple/Universal Community Help, who are launching this book, are creating history, providing support counselling to the needy at their Temple/UCH along with the training of support counsellors The recent 26.12.2004 Tsunami disaster in Asia did attract global empathy, help in cash and kind poured in, which seemed to generate a new phase of understanding among the opponents of the internal conflict in Sri Lanka. However, the situation has deteriorated and things are back again to square one.

The dove of Peace continues to hover ever so slowly above Sri Lanka and daily negative news abounds with violence, abductions and assassinations. I sincerely hope that my words will help to awaken more awareness and interest among the powerful nations of the world and the Mass Media. I strongly feel that material help alone, is never sufficient. It is great that this concept was recently stressed in his presentation, by Psychiatrist Dr.Daya Somasunderam, rendering selfless service in the University and the Teaching Hospital at Jaffna, when he participated in the Trauma & Global Mental Health Conference in Toronto by invitation in May 2005.

I wrote a Tamil Dance Drama, 'The Dawn of Thamil Eelam' long ago in 1987 when I lived in Jaffna amidst the war and the patrolling soldiers. I have included it as the final poem of section Two, in this collection and do hope and pray that my dream will become a reality soon. Every nation must actively participate in the ongoing Peace Processes and initiate appropriate efforts to ensure Peace with Justice all over the world, especially in my war-torn motherland, Sri Lanka stumbling under the tsunami disaster, a shaky Cease-fire and prolonging Peace Negotiations.

Lalitha Brodie
E mail: lalitha.brodie022@sympatico.ca
Lalitha Brodie's Photo by Irene Borins Ash
www.ireneborins.ash.com
lbaging@look.ca

I. SPIRITUAL

1. ADORATION

Sprouting bud and pirouetting birdsong
herald the dawn of yet another spring.
My brimming heart with adoration does sing
the glory of God! My creator! My king!
Thanks my Lord, for giving me the strength
to forge forward, battling against every obstacle
with the attitude to accept both pleasure and pain.
I realize that events in life come to teach us lessons
and as the great Archer, who bends me as a bow
You have already destined it, and made me aware
that the more I bend, the further will fly my arrow!

My Lord! I no longer have a name or form
for You. However, when I introvert, meditate
and try to touch my core, at long last I've come
to realize, that your spark is not only within me,
but in everyone else too! I sense Your benevolent
presence in every single thing that exists
in Your creation, both inside and outside!
I too am a component of that inimitable
Power, The Omnipresent Whole That Is You!

You are the eternal Light reigning supreme!
You guided me into Sukyo Mahikari in 1992.
Your radiant flame now grants light
in abundance, directing my path as an instrument
to radiate True Light dispelling darkness,
while life continues to unfold around me.
Praise and adoration to You My Lord!
Your healing hand has removed the sting
of disability, that severe osteoporosis would bring!
Swift with song, my spirit soars on a silvery wing
Savouring the melodious bells of Your blessing
that yet another new home in Canada will ring.

2. BHAGAVAN SRI SATHIYA SAI BABA

I was busy coping with my family and content
when quite uninvited, You intruded into my life in
1971, with your discourses in"Sathiya Sai Speaks!"
To effect any change in anyone is so very difficult,
but somehow You slowly managed to change me!
Doubting me! saying My whole outlook and course of
life! I reverently accepted You as my preceptor and
Guru in 1972, when you first smilingly walked up to
bless me, "I am glad you've come!" After which,
like a magnet, you daily draw me to Yourself
in my visualisations, and have made me
visit You eight times in India!
However, with the increasing crowds of devotees,
though I am aware of your grace and have touched
your feet, You have never spoken to me again!

The daily expanding face of your abode Puttaparthi,
with the enormous pastel iced-cake like structures,
the integrated Free Education at all Your Colleges
which raise self-esteem by nurturing human values,
now accepted and taught in every school in India.
Your astounding, outreach of Social Service
and free Medi-care at Your two world class
Super Specialty Hospitals. Your dedication

to globally nurture the spirituality of humanity.
The sanctity, peace and joy that always surround
you. And best of all, your miraculous ability
to know, touch, help and in addition, enhance
the life of every single individual seeker,
speak volumes for You, Your life and Your
message! When I glance back, I marvel
at the complete turn that my life has taken
since your intervention and my cup
overflows with gratitude and joy!

3. THE WHOLE

I continue my progress, coping with the trials
and tribulations of life
The exacting tests which everyone
without exception has to experience,
to proceed on the pilgrim's way, daily
becoming more and more aware
of the power of God within, guiding me!
My new life in hospitable Canada
affirms that I too am but an infinitesimal
particle of that Great Cosmic Whole,

the great Power that is God, who commands
and miraculously weaves together
this vibrant vast mosaic of the universe.

My Lord! Please grant me the vision, foresight,
fortitude and the strength, to never look back
complain and linger, but to always accept
and act in the Here and the Now.
To always, remember that unconditional
love, peace, self-esteem, contentment,
and happiness have to always first spring
from inside me! Happiness is a by-product
of our thoughts, emotions, words and deeds
and cannot be given to us by others,
or bought from outside. Like a butterfly
joy will fly away if chased, but will
return on its own with introversion, when
the ego is erased and the self is forgotten.
Please help me to never harbour grudges and
hatred but also as an offender myself, learn
to forgive, forget and become free, to accept
and continue in my environment, and achieve
the very best that I possibly can, in all my
endeavours amongst my allotted circle of relationships.

4. ACCEPTANCE

Winter has arrived once again with sleet and snow
painting pure white the face of Ontario,
and the stinging wind outside makes me shiver
and shudder. I know that change is essential
for all growth in life. In the ceaseless procession
of the ever-changing seasons, winter has its own
beauty too without which, autumn, spring and
summer will each lose its special charm, but still. . . .

In my motherland, the tiny tropical isle of
Sri Lanka, I yet remember, learning in junior
geography class to name the great Canadian
lakes on the map of the world! Though then,
I just couldn't imagine the coniferous trees
jostling the icicles nor how the Eskimos could
build their cosy igloos! Life does unfold full of
surprising twists and turns! I never dreamed
that in 1992, I would flee Jaffna and arrive
in Toronto! Of course, I first felt homesick
and pined for my habitual haunts.
Now, although my heart yet weeps for my war
ravaged land, the muffled cries, and the stifled
sufferings of my beloved brethren,
entwined in the relentless coils of the catastrophe
of continuing warfare, at long last I realise,
that though it is not always quite clear,
life continues to unfold as destined,

to fulfil the eternal cosmic plan.
This benefactor that is Canada, offering shelter
with safety to me and my people, is my new home
and refuge, and I bow my head with a heart
brimming with grateful acceptance!

5. CREATION

With persistence I centred once again amidst
contemplation, deep into the realm of visualization
and meditation, perplexed by the eternal
unanswerable questions and the rumination
on the mysteries of life, creation
and the veiled obscure purpose of life ...
Who am I? From where did I come?
Why am I really here now?
And whither do I go from here?
Why is it so difficult for me, to passively accept
the answers of earlier prophets, saints and seers?
Surely this marvel of the spirit, mind,
psyche, intellect, emotions and the body
has not been created to only eat, drink, make
merry, beget offspring, amass wealth wisdom,
name, fame, power, and then fade, wither and die?

As a seeker, I delved into various faiths and
religions known and unknown, as best as I could.
Instinct confirms the presence of God

like the pervasive power of the unseen wind.
Manmade religions, surging rivers seeking to merge
into the common sea of bliss, The Divine,
that One Omnipotent Power That is God,
identified and adored in various traditional forms
and by numerous names to suit the need
of each and every individual seeker. . .

Siva, Allah, Jesus, Mary, Su, Sukyo Mahikari,
Menorah, Zeus, Zoroaster, Sufi, Guru Nanak,
Mahavira, Odin, Inti, Ra, Krishna, Rama, Kabir,
Shamash, Buddah, Aten, Ramakrishna, Yogananda,
Vivekananda, Osho, Sri Vasudeva, Maharaji, Yogi
Satyam, Amirthananthamayi, Sathya Sai Baba
But beloved God Almighty, One and Only!
How great, how great Thou art my Lord!
How great are Thy power and Thy glory!
There is no single face, body or mind like another,
Never a similar story, stone, sprout or summer.
No identical thought, action or even laughter.
To create this massive mosaic of such glorious
diversity, command it, reign uncontested
and supreme, how great Thou art!
My Lord, How great Thou art!
and how very little we understand
of Thy inscrutable ways!
With these thoughts pervading my mind,
I fell fast asleep and dreamed . . .

Divine handiwork the Universe watched with awed
reverence, as the timeless Lord Siva*, Hindu king
of the heavens, cobras adorned, holy ash and tiger
skin clad, with the crescent moon and the river
Ganges flowing forth from his matted locks, atop
worlds highest Himalayan peak icebound
Mount Everest, the abode of the immortal Devas,
Kailash, sat in meditation long silent and still,
drinking from the cup of self to His fill . . .

At last, Thriyambaha* opened His three eyes
and beheld the outcome of his intense
concentration. "Oh! What a shame!
Is this all? This is but a ball of barren soil!
The planet earth! Of what use can this be?"
With great disappointment and utter dismay
Abinath* flung that orb out into the void
of the cosmos and silently watched,
as the world revolved and rotated away.

Lalitha

30

At the flash of a sudden insight, Sambasiva*
Beckoned His better half, Umadevi*
"Behold the Bhuloka, that smooth sphere twirling
afar? Go forth! See what you can do with it!"
Goddess Parvathy*, full of power and grace,
stepped on the sterile earth, spinning in space.
Energetically Kali* toiled, digging hill and dale,
plateau and plain, waterfall and mountain.
The salty sea, spring, stream, river, desert, oasis
and fountain. Deftly Durga* sculptured the face
of the earth with superb skill, and joined her Lord
in the ceaseless eternal cosmic dance with mirth.

Resplendent Lakshmi on the red lotus, bestower
of wealth, was the red clad Goddess, Nadarajah*
sent next. With one sweep of Her bounteous hand
Sri Devi made the whole wide world fertile
with grain, tree, flower, seed, fruit, yam and creeper
vegetable, cotton, cocoa, coffee, tea and rubber
dawn, dusk, noon, sunset and the evening shower
Thirumagal did pierce deep into the bowels of the
earth, and buried all the rare multi-fold treasures.
copper, iron, slate, granite, gold and silver
the nine precious gems and diamonds aglitter.

Surprised, elated and excited with this quick
progress, Neelakanda* next despatched the Goddess
of wisdom. White clad and serene on the white
lotus, Devi Saraswathy. With the first twang of

31

Sarathe's vina string the silence ceased, and in
melody, the world did sing with music and sound.
'Om'intoned the wind! Thunder clapped!
'Pitter patter'sang the rain! Brooks rippled merrily
and waves roared! Next, with artistic brush
and multihued paint, fragrant flowers, the rainbow,
black rock and brown sod, shades of green
to the creepers, ferns, leaves and the grass.
The sea and sky blue, with clouds as white as glass
Kalaimagal did bestow beauty, colour
and sound to every possible thing!

Utterly pleased with this excellent artistic tapestry
of the talented consorts of the Hindu Trinity,
the facets of the Supreme, Brahma, Vishnu and Siva
Mahadeva* took time, exploited His skill and power
and created the first form of life, the amoeba.
At once the amoeba systematically split in two
and the pair simply floated away with never
a look behind! Then pair by pair Paramasiva*
did continue to create the myriads of each and every
varied form of life. Mite, fish, insect, bird, animal,
reptile and watched with mounting impatience
as they all hurried away, busy as ever
in their eternal quest for food, pleasure and power.

Utterly disillusioned Maheswara* exclaimed,
'As my last effort, I will coerce my utmost power
and create the human beings, man and woman

32

in my image, with my divine spark within as their
conscience and bless them with the sixth sense!'
Lo and behold! The first homo-sapiens Adam
and Eve, the inimitable wondrous miracle of creation
stood before the splendorous Sivasambo*.
They looked around and up at Haran's* benevolent
face and instinctively knew how to win Sathasiva's*
grace. Down they prostrated at His lotus feet
with thanks, love, worship, praise and adoration.

Gratified and glad, the great God Gangatharan*
blessed them, "As long as you both strive to live
with Truth, Love, Peace, Righteousness and
Non-violence, and ensure that the three facets
of humanity, The Body, Mind and the Spirit
are nurtured in balanced growth, Health, Wealth,
Harmony and Happiness will be yours!
Go forth with joy, into this wide wonderful world!
Procreate your descendants, march forward in
honest endeavour toward the aim of
Self Actualisation, and reach the true goal of life,
Self Realisation! Henceforth Brahma will be in
charge of creation! Avatars of Vishnu will take
human birth, time and time again to nurture
the growth of righteousness on earth."

The first human couple, Adam and Eve were amazed!
At the magnificent world around them, they gazed.
It was beautiful and busy, bustling with harmony

and joy. Happy and content, away they went with peace and started the ceaseless cycle of human life.

However, little by little things began to change and go awry. The ego and the insatiable desires of their fickle mind, instigated the humans to ignore and neglect the spirit and pamper only their body and every whim of the restless mind and emotions. Seeking selfish pleasure, money, material possessions and power became the one and only goal of life of every single human being.
Sin multiplied, righteousness declined, evil prospered and now we are daily confronted with the result as the negative holocaust of envy, malice, anger, hatred, crime, robbery, rape, revenge, murder and war, that roam unfettered, hand in hand inside every single individual human heart!
It is said, 'though it may not be now clear to thee, the world is unfolding as it should.' But is it really? It is indeed frightening, to see this lack of truth, unconditional love, right conduct, empathy and two-way communication in all manners of human relationships and the futile misery of endless war and destruction, that unfortunately plague and torment our globe today. If we can only become aware, accept, change, rectify our mistakes and ensure that the spirit, mind and the body are nurtured simultaneously from childhood, to grow and blossom together in balanced harmony,

will not that be the first step, to make certain
that even at this stage, all the misery besetting
human life and relationships will vanish and
peace and joy on earth will prevail again?

My Lord! My Lord! My Beloved Lord!
Please make it easier for every one of us to
realise that the goal of life is indeed attaining
Heaven. However this Heaven is not an exalted
abode overflowing with the nectar of ambrosia,
bliss and immortality. Heaven is really an
awareness of the enlightened state of the human
mind, brimming with true selfless Love
without the ego of the me and the mine.
God and Heaven are Really Within Us
and Within the Reach of Every One of Us!
My Lord! Please help us one and all
to introvert, look within ourselves,
watch our minds and start the trek
toward this state of mind, that is Heaven.
Thank you my Lord, for so abundantly
blessing us, with this rare opportunity
of human birth. Please do help, guide
and lead us on to the victorious end
of every single pilgrim's way.

*A few of the numerous names of
Lord Siva and his consort Umathevi.
1995

6. KRIYA YOGA & YOGI SATYAM
10.4.2004

Thank you dear Guruji Yogi Satyam
for initiating me into Kriya Yoga
in June 2002 in Toronto, Canada.
I had earlier particularly focused
only on my mind and spirit
but I was led to you in good time
to also nurture my crippled body
that I had neglected for so long
till osteoporosis robbed me of
46% of my bone density
and scoliosis curved and made me
shorter by a good five inches!

I yet feel the fragrance of knowledge,
well-being, peace and joy that I gained
from your Kriya Yoga sessions
four times daily during my 45 day retreat
at your Allahabad Ashram in Jan. 2004.
You did really help Guruji, to nurture
my mind, emotions, body and spirit
towards healthy, balanced growth.
I now feel so full of energy
and am really open and more aware!
I know that you, your family and disciples

have dedicated yourselves heart body and soul
to uplift the lives of humanity worldwide
by disseminating the science of Kriya Yoga.

I had read The Autobiography of A Yogi
over thirty years ago, but only now I realize
its true value and significance.
Ancient Kriya Yoga, re-introduced
by the immortal Maha Avathar Babaji,
nurtured by Paramahamsa Yoganandha,
is now in your hands for propagation!
It was a marvellous experience to camp out
on the dry bed of the mighty river Ganges
and participate in the Magh Mela 2004!
Please do visit Sri Lanka and introduce
Kriya Yoga so that the our people
too can enjoy its benefits and benediction.

20.4.2004
I have just returned from visiting Kataragama
after twenty years. The vicinity of this
earlier oft-visited temple has indeed changed
radically, but it is lovely to yet feel the pulsing
devotion of the ardent hoards of increased Hindu,
Buddist and Muslim devotees both young and old,
gaining grace from our beloved Lord Murugan
and other Hindu deities, as this ancient hallowed
shrine continues to nurture spirituality in Sri Lanka.

I feel the grace of God Almighty enveloping me
when at Kataragama, Sri Jhoshi, Chief Hindu Priest
for over four decades at the Vinayagar temple,
somehow recognizes and blesses me on his own
with prasad. My daughter shows me the Kriya
Peedam with the statue and photograph of the
death-less Maha-Avathar Babaji, which I never
noticed during our countless pilgrimages earlier!

What a miraculous coincidence this is
when I am trying to propagate Kriya Yoga
in Sri Lanka! I race back to the priest again
and he confirms that the ever youthful Babaji
had earlier lived in Viputhimalai, Kataragama.
Babaji now abides in the Himalayas, and yet
reveals himself to chosen devotees at Maghmela
in-between and Kumbamela every twelve years,
those massive spiritual festivals that in rotation
adorn Harithwar, Ujjayani, Naazic and Sangam.

I joined Yogi Satyam at Magh Mela near holy
Sangam, the triple conjunction of rivers Ganga,
Jamuna and Saraswathy. Hindu Mythology
says, that after the churning of the ocean of milk
by the celestial Devas and enemy Demons,
King Indra's son Sayanthan, fleeing from pursuit
with the chalice of ambrosia, rested in four places
to quench his thirst with the nectar. The few

drops that then spilled near these four rivers
sanctified the waters, which wash off the sins
of all individuals who bathe in them at the proper
astrological hour! You too may tend to believe
this myth, when you see the massive hoards of
trekking pilgrims bathing at these holy rivers!

20.5.2004
Melbourne - Australia
I yet feel so vibrant and young at heart
though I will be seventy years old this year!
How blest I am to thus travel, out of the blue,
almost around the world, even Australia too!
I find that with its mild weather patterns
Melbourne is indeed a glorious place.
I grab the opportunity and speak at
The Senior Tamil Centre, Victoria
about the benefits of practicing Kriya Yoga!
They are very interested and I do hope that
they will invite Yogi Satyam to teach them.

Greater Toronto, Canada
It is lovely to meet Sri Yogi Satyam
on home ground once again!
At his arrival, I had the privilege
of presenting him to receptive listeners
of Canadian International Tamil Radio
in my regular program, to try and help

Balanced Individual Personal Growth
of the Spirit, Mind, Emotions and Body.
More and more crowds are now
daily flocking to imbibe the science
of Kriya Yoga from his entirely free
sessions in Ontario in different locations
that continue till December 2004.
www.kriyayoga-yogisatyam.org

7.THE ETERNAL CYCLE

Twin baby brothers
cocooned, crowded
and comfortless
inside the womb
of their pregnant mother . . .

Protested one, to the other
"Hey! Stop kicking!"
"Stop shouting," came the retort
"I feel that it's now time
for the big change!
We will soon be out in flight
to see the bright light
and the face of our dear mother!"
"Hah! What imagination!"
Scoffed the first.

40

"Flight? Light? Mother? What else?
What more can there be
than this hospitable haven?
We are safe and sound here
and so well cared for!
Stop your daydreaming
and get back to sleep!

On the day of the next full moon
were born the twins, minutes apart,
screaming with anger and fear,
confronted by the unexpected change . . .

However, once born we learn to accept
and try very hard to cope and adjust
to continuing cycles of pleasure and pain
and the changes in our transient lives.
But when the time does arrive at last
for our eternal spirit to depart
discarding the cloak of this worn out body
why do we find it so difficult
to realise, understand and accept
that it is again the age-old story
of history, repeating itself?

June 1997

II. THAMIL EELAM

8. THE ANNIVERSARY

With the dawn of New Year 1998, begins our year
long celebration of the Tenth Anniversary of the
pioneer, The Older Women's Network, Ontario,
to commemorate our joint efforts through thick
and thin, this our very first decade! Our tall
and stately new OWN Housing Co-op.
Pierces the Toronto skyline, proclaiming our power!
An eternal symbol to demonstrate our success
of increasing recognition and achievement in
meeting all needs of every Canadian older woman!

After the recent observance of the 50th anniversary
of the Universal Declaration of Human Rights
My mind darts back to our
Mothers' Front, Jaffna
Sri Lanka, also initiated a
decade ago, to voice our
protests against the despotic
state of Sri Lanka!

We mothers rose against the
unwarranted arrests
and merciless torture of our
innocent youth.

43

The 1948 Disenfranchisement of a million Tamils.
The suppression in 1956 of our mother tongue Tamil,
when Sinhalese was made the only official language.
The unjust standardisation of University Entrance
on no merit but area basis, resulting in lost
hopes and the never-ending exodus of Tamil brain
drain. The blatant state aided colonization of the
fringes of the North and the East. The communal
violence unleashed against the Tamils all over the
isle again and again, while the state watched, when
more than three thousand Tamil civilians were
brutally slaughtered and property worth millions
wantonly destroyed in the ethnic riots.
The destruction of our ancient Hindu temples, holy
churches, hospitals, schools and civilian homes by
indiscriminate aerial bombs and artillery shells
from more than 250 army camps surrounding us.
The pre-planned burning of the best in the East
Jaffna Public Library in 1981. The tyranny of
continuing multi-media censorship. The systematic
oppression and denial of our basic human rights
along with forty other basic essentials . . .
What and what we Tamil mothers accomplished!
We organized slogan shouting long protest marches.
Sit down silent protest fasts with fiery placards
under umbrellas in the blazing sun, in front of the

Govt. Secretariat. We invaded all offices one day, sat in front of the main officers and even managed to bring all Govt. functions to a complete standstill!

With the aid of The Friend in Need Society, Colombo, The overall Jaffna President Themba Gunanayagam, Secy.Rene Yoganathan, the two unselfish live wires Dr.Mrs.Ganeshamoorthy, Dr.Mrs.Theivendran, Ganesh Bala, Shanthi Sivaps and I as president Chundikuli, initiated the first and only low-cost Artificial Leg Jaipur Foot Project in Jaffna. We still distribute free handmade limbs to the victims of war and the terrible civilian toll of landmine blasts, which help the needy to walk with hope once again.

In 1989 with the help of Quaker Peace, NORAD and Befrienders International, Rev.Dr.Selvaratnam, Rev.Damian, Dr.Daya Somasunderam, some other caring professionals and I from The Mothers' Front, joined to create Shanthiyaham, introducing the first and only Psychological Counselling Centre serving the North. Both these essential services yet continue to function amidst the war, in spite of the entire, mind-boggling setbacks!

News from the warfront is more and more scarce
now amidst severe fighting, in the latest "Do or
Die" Military Operation, "Victory Assured"!
The State even more strictly censors the
Multimedia, after the invading Sri Lankan Army
ousted control of Jaffna in October 1995 and
paints a rosy picture of liberating the Tamils!
But our people are mortally scared of the merciless
rule of the gun, tired of the frequent Army
Checkpoints, arrests, detainments, rapes and murder
of our school children, and still attempt to flee
Jaffna, in spite of all the state propaganda!
Sri Lanka prepares to celebrate the 50th anniversary
of Independence on February 4, 1998.
The State is trying hard to win the Tamils over,
with Municipal Elections, promises to reinstate the
burnt Public Library and other structures . . .

Temples, Churches, Schools, Libraries and houses
can be rebuilt. But the irreplaceable lost lives,
ancient Olas and rare manuscripts? Are these
fragile attempts sufficient, to quench the thirst
for freedom and win back the trust and lost
goodwill of our suppressed languishing people?

9. MUSINGS . . .

It's November 1996, late autumn in Toronto.
I watch silently in anguished dismay
as the eternal conflict between the good
and the bad, daily escalates higher and higher . . .

The Devil that is violence continues his carnage
drunk with lust and power, pampering only the
body, spreading his dance of death and destruction
to grimace in triumph everywhere. In families,
The Caribana, Air-flights, Ireland, Iraq, Zaire, Bosnia,
Rwanda, Mid-East, Arabia, Atlanta, Sri Lanka!
Oh! What is this? Why . . .Why . . . Why?

Negative thoughts when un-harnessed,
spawn negative emotions and actions.
Hatred, revenge, crimes, gunfire, bomb blasts,
missiles and wars stalk every nook and corner
and no place in the world seems safe now
in spite of every possible precaution.
The Multi-media tries to hurdle censorship,
to report the unending headline holocausts.
We gasp in horror only for the moment,
manage to don masks, push our feelings aside

and uncaring continue, trying to only cope
with the trivialities of our own selfish lives.
What can, and what should every one of us do
to prevent the birth, growth and spread
of this traumatic terror, that is violence?
We spend so much of effort, time and money
on the Olympics and the Nobel Prize
to encourage, recognize, admire and applaud
excellence of the Body and the Mind.
However, sadly neglected pines the Spirit . . .

Self-awareness and change to boost basic values
Love, Truth, Right Conduct, Non-violence
and Peace will aid personal growth,
raise individual self-esteem, which will in turn
dispel the need for abuse and violence to exert
power and control over the other to feel happy.
I believe that nurturing Individual Personal
Growth is the best way to build a solid foundation
to eradicate all negativity and help to universally
create healthy families, progressive communities,
united nations and a harmonious humanity.
Why not we introvert, touch our core and seek...
My Messiah Complex has reared its head once
again and given words to my ceaseless thoughts!
Oh! If only my words could have wings . . .

10. UNITY IN DIVERSITY

Travelling the Toronto TTC with passengers
of a multicultural flare
I daily marvel at the well synchronised harmony
evident everywhere.
Always striving hard to preserve each and every
single individual identity
While yet managing to promote peace and harmony
despite all the diversity!
How is it that just two factions in tiny Sri-Lanka
The Tamil and the Sinhalese, find it so difficult
and cannot resolve their escalating conflict
to start negotiations towards peace with justice?
1992

11. PEACE ON EARTH

November 1995 - Its Military 'Operation Sunshine'!
My folks have fled Jaffna in fear! The Sri Lankan
army has hoisted its flag in my ghost hometown!
Thousands are refugees, trekking like in Rwanda,
but all news is effectively censored by the State!
However, the multimedia is
permitted to report
The Central Bank bomb-blast in
Colombo! Will they never stop this
revenge seeking violence?

49

Astronomers sight two brand new planets
and the world is now wide-eyed with wonder!
Why not we learn to introvert and look
at the vast unexplored universe of our mind?
Watch it, and learn to love, trust and be at peace
first of all with our very own selves
so that we can begin to radiate love, self-esteem
empathy and understanding to everyone around us.
When this essential awareness kindles and awakens
in us, the urgent need to prevent the growth
and spread of unjust evil on earth, escalate efforts
to nurture the harmonious growth of the Spirit too,
along with the Mind and the Body, surely
the change in our attitudes, habits and actions
will ensure that Health, Wealth, Happiness
and PEACE will reign supreme amongst us all.

12. MARTYR   DILEEPAN – 1987

Curled up on the bed in the small shed you lay
in front of the Nallur Temple in Jafffna, Sri Lanka.
Fanatically determined to prolong your protest fast
till death, if the rulers failed to meet your
five requests for the cause of Tamil Eelam

I sat there on the ground, along
with the thousands
around you keeping vigil, while our
people filed past

non-stop with tears and prayers that the word would
come. I never ever dreamed that your non-violent effort
would be in vain and we would lose
one such as you, beloved Dileepa!

You, the 26-year-old medical college dropout!
You, the charismatic Leader of Youth!
You, the eloquent orator with the fiery tongue!
You, who chose to use the non-violent weapon
of the total fast, like a Gandhi!
Oh! You kept your word, Dileepa!
You kept your word and faded and withered
before our very eyes, without even a sip
of water for thirteen days!
Awaiting the word, which never did come
from the heartless rulers.
They ignored your extended hand
for peace and chose to keep silent.
And you, the first martyr for the Tamil Cause
slowly withered and died sacrificing yourself,
like a candle in the wind,
bequeathing your mortal frame
for medical research

Isn't the will to survive paramount in creation?
Oh! Do tell me Dileepa! Tell me!
In the prime of youth, how did you manage
to triumph over your basic needs? Your instincts?

Not even a drop of water did you ask for!
Your strict instructions were not to be fed
intravenously, even after you lost consciousness!

The picture of your resolute face still flashes forth
when I find myself unable to bear thirst and hunger.
I find it so very difficult to waste anything now, food,
drinks or even paper, and am criticised lots of
times for these war-conditioned habits of mine.
People would understand this more, if only they had
lived amidst the traumatic terror that is a war . . .

13. PEACE AND HOPE

We Tamils, hail from a war ravaged land
Tamil Eelam, crowning the North
and embracing the east
of the emerald isle, that is Sri Lanka.
Is it wrong for us to envision Freedom?
and long for an independent state of our own?
But we are oppressed and denied basic human
rights and our cities still shudder under siege!
Well more than one hundred and seventy
thousand of us, have fled our beloved
Motherland and sought refuge in this
multicultural, hospitable
haven that is Canada.

Unexpectedly uprooted from habitual haunts
I keep busy, trying to expand my horizons
and cope with this entirely new way of life.
However memory pictures, vivid as ever
haunt me and often flash forth in my mind's eye . .

The dreaded drone of the helicopter hornet
heralding the pot-bellied bombers, that dive
deep like giant pregnant dragonflies
that lay their seven eggs in flight!
Followed by the blinding flash and the
deafening blast, of death and destruction,
driving us to huddle in fear in bunkers
dug inside the bosom of the earth!

The handsome face of dear nephew Sasi
Sweet sixteen, fair, tall and lanky
Gone without even a funeral
Killed in combat at Killinochchi . . .

That artillery shell from the Palaly Army Camp
suddenly whizzing over our roof
to destroy neighbour Muthuthamby's house
killing him, son and daughter in a split second,
the loss that wife Yoga, yet suicidal and
grieving in Toronto, cannot still get over . . .

Dark and swarthy Amerasingam
stretched inert, ignorant and unaware
on the crowded Jaffna Hospital floor,
paralysed neck down with spinal injury,
but with the glint of hope in his eyes,
that clever surgeon Ganesh, will somehow
heal and make him walk once again . . .

The pretty sad eyed university student Selva,
(who later disappeared!) at our Shanthiyaham
Centre, Jaffna, remembering forcibly held down
by two, while five heartless IPKF soldiers raped her...

That lovely teen-aged schoolgirl Chrishanthi,
disappearing after detention at the army check-point,
the distraught mother and neighbour venturing
to investigate too vanish, all three later found
raped, killed and buried by Sri Lankan soldiers!

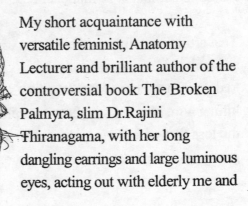 My short acquaintance with
versatile feminist, Anatomy
Lecturer and brilliant author of the
controversial book The Broken
Palmyra, slim Dr.Rajini
Thiranagama, with her long
dangling earrings and large luminous
eyes, acting out with elderly me and

six undergraduates the topical play "Kitchen Gossip"
about the travails of war and the pathetic plight of
raped women, to the packed audience
on university stage, for the first and the last time,

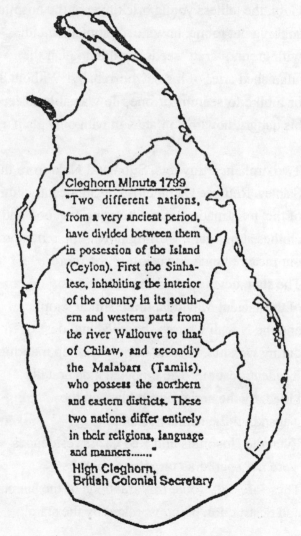

Cleghorn Minute 1799
"Two different nations,
from a very ancient period,
have divided between them
in possession of the Island
(Ceylon). First the Sinhalese, inhabiting the interior
of the country in its south-
ern and western parts from
the river Wallouve to that
of Chilaw, and secondly
the Malabars (Tamils),
who possess the northern
and eastern districts. These
two nations differ entirely
in their religions, language
and manners......."
High Cleghorn,
British Colonial Secretary

so cruelly assassinated soon afterwards in her prime,
by unknown gunmen as she cycled home
alone from the Jaffna university!

Gobi, the jobless young bricklayer at the hospital
sobbing out to me, how he attempted suicide
with ground 'arali' seeds, unable to bear the
anguished cries of his newborn baby! Without a job
or a bike to search for one, he was able to feed
his hungry, howling infant son with only plain tea!

Two orphaned tiny tots, Suba and Nala from the
Stanley Refugee Camp close by. innocent victims
of the man-made famine, begging for food and
clothes at our gate, wolfing down the remnants of
our meagre lunch and asking   for more . . .
The slain devotees and the old Priests
of the ancient Maviddapuram Hindu temple
and the Navali Church, bombed and destroyed
during worship, in spite of bold rooftop markings
for identification. The innocent kids brutally
killed, by the aerial bomb blast on the
Nagarkovil Elementary school.
Even the Hospitals and Red Cross residences
were not spared as targets for bombs!
These are only some tiny fractions of the havoc
and destruction being wreaked by the state!

The two well-known Assistant Govt.Agents
Balasingham and Kamala Sivasithamparam
en-route to Point Pedro on duty,
stopping the jeep to change a flat tyre.
One stepped on a roadside landmine,
the other ran to help him and she too fell,
both simultaneously losing their legs in agony.
Only to later rise from their irreparable loss
as exemplary volunteer leaders
to serve other amputees, at the Chundikuli
Mother's Front Jaipur Leg Workshop.

The pain contorted face of innocent Kanthi,
ten years old, with third degree burns!
Another victim of the kerosene oil
bottle lamp tragedies - one of the results
of the denial of basic essentials to the war zones.
Electricity, Fuel, Transport, Communications
Medicare, Nutrition, Sanitation, Batteries, Plastic,
Candles and even Matches among forty others . . .

Oh! I have seen the terror of what is war!
Life for life! Limb for limb! Eye for eye!
As usual in war, the opponents continue to cry!
Will the revenge seeking conflict never cease?
Until everyone turns cripple or blind?

A whole young generation on both sides is gone!
While they wail for their lost sons
they gloat over the victory
after killing similar sons of the other . . .
Oh! I feel so sad and powerless
that I do nothing else to help, but only write . . .

Peace! Peace! Oh elusive peace!
Where! Oh! Where are you?
We seek you and we yearn for you!
Why are you so difficult to find?
Is it because you want to first ensure
that every one of us should turn and look within
and learn to be at peace with our very own selves?
so that we can fill our hearts and minds
with those essential basic human values
Love, Truth, Non-violence and Empathy,
that will lead us toward Right Conduct,
curb the ego of the me and the mine,
place a ceiling on desires for control and power
and nurture our starving spirit too
along with the body and the mind
in balanced harmony from childhood
so that every single one of us can hope that
YOU, THE GREAT POWER THAT IS PEACE
will reign supreme in every human heart

to overflow and spread your healing balm
in all the nooks and corners of the troubled world.

March 1995
Hark! There is a glimmer of light!
At last a cease-fire has been declared!
Negotiations are now in progress in Sri Lanka
too as in all other countries at war!
Oh! Come! You, The United Nations!
The Mighty Leaders of the World!
And the powerful Multimedia!
We urgently need your support and help now
to ensure that this dawn of Hope of Peace
With Justice is appropriately tended
to blossom forth fully into reality
to spread peace and joy in Sri Lanka
and every country in the whole wide world!

Oh! How disappointing! It is so unfortunate!
Peace negotiations have collapsed!
War! Fierce war has broken out once again!
Our people suffer untold misery and hardships
once again, as homeless refugees in our own land.
They are unfortunate pawns in this continuing
conflict, suffering death, and devastating
destruction, which relentlessly torments our
beloved land.

It is a pity, that media censorship muffles the truth
and the world remains unaware of our plight!
We reach out, and raise our voices together!
We cry out and appeal to you, one and all!
Please, please pay attention, intervene,
Initiate all what is possible and essential
and do please help us to gain Peace With Justice!

 *All episodes are true
experiences.
Published by
FRIENDS OF RWANDA Toronto in 1995.

14. THE STANLEY REFUGEE CAMP
October 1987

We welcome The Indian Peace Keeping Force into
Jaffna with open arms! We do believe that they
would mediate, settle the conflict and bring peace
between the Government and the Tamil LTTE, but
things go terribly wrong!
The trusted neighbour and friend turns into a formidable
foe! Bombs and shells join in, as the IPKF soldiers
advance into Jaffna from several sides, shooting left
right and centre!
We hide under our beds in fear that whole night
to escape the non-stop gunfire pelting our walls.
"Leave your homes and get to Stanley College',
barks the army loudspeaker the next morning!
More than ten thousand of us, Ariyalai civilians
run into the 800 student strong Stanley College,
creating a crowded make-shift refugee camp
sans electricity, running water, and all other essentials!

The army vehicles patrol early next morning.
We are herded to the grounds with up-raised arms
under the blazing sun, and not one dares to complain!
The face covered 'Thaliarty' spies, watch us closely
as we file past. If he nods and identifies trespassers
the unfortunate ones are handcuffed and removed!

Quite unaware that soldiers occupy our houses
several neighbours going home to their washrooms
fall, including pretty Rani, shot dead by the sentries.
A teenager, is taken and the mother clings to me for
help!

After three unbearable days, the stench of rotting
corpses around us, compels us, five older women to
venture towards the army camp, hoisting a large white
SOS flag amidst two poles shouting 'Help!, Help!"
The wary North Indian soldiers appear and advance
slowly towards us stooping with pointed rifles.
With raised arms I first request the release
of the teen-ager. Luckily one soldier knows Tamil
and replies that he is safe and to talk to the commander.
I ask permission to cremate the dead at the same
spots, but the exchange is unexpectedly interrupted!
They see a man in the distance, panic that we are
LTTE decoys and start thundering a volley of
bullets! Both the soldiers and we scatter and run for
our lives! I realise my mistake in not writing
down our requests in a letter to the Commander!!

The next morning the captured boy's mother,
relatives of the dead and I go to the main army
camp and meet young commander Rakesh Dube.
I shout out blaming him for all the death and

destruction they have caused, but he patiently
listens to my outburst! He permits the cremations.
He wants the mother and me to accompany the
soldiers on foot to the temple to get the boy.
On our way, the captain kicks open the door
and we gather rice, lentils, milk powder etc
from the co-op store in a cart for the camp.

Gentle Dr.Pushpanathan and Ariyalai nurses help
me to set up a Medical clinic. Hospital Volunteers
bring us essential supplies and we are able to treat
victims of gunshots, shell fire and bomb blasts.
A baby is born in the middle of the night
by coconut oil lamp light (Where is that child now?)

Rice and vegetables are cooked together in the large
college cauldrons on open fire in the compound.
Pit latrines are erected and the 25 feet deep well
with the coconut palm well-sweep, provides the never
ending supply of fresh water. After about ten days
some of us return home but the majority choose
 the safety of the Nallur Temple refugee camp.

When things settle down, the IPKF army occupies
Stanley College and the commander starts visiting us
at No.4 Brodie Lane. There is a convoy of soldiers

on guard around our house with arms during these visits. He starts coming more often, calling me and my husband Ma and Pa! There is severe food shortage. Tongues start wagging that he brings us bags of foodstuff! In the end I have to ask him to stop the visits as our lives are in danger. He complies!

I now marvel at our resilience during those days of dreadful danger and such dire need. No foodstuff, fuel or medicines came into Jaffna, but all of us somehow or other managed to survive! Similarly, time and time again so many relationships step into our lives to teach us lessons. When we complete our learning and the need ceases, the relationships too vanish!

15. AHILAN
5.5.1970 – 10.5.1989

You were barely nineteen, beloved Ahilan
when you fell victim to bullets of heartless
assassins! You, the epitome of excellence
of Tamil youth! The promising all-round winner
at St.Johns' College! Precious only child
of veteran journalist Thiruchelvam and Ranji!

64

I yet remember the grief and sympathy
that spurted forth from every single
individual person in Jaffna, at your
massive funeral!
Your paternal grandfather died of a broken heart
two weeks after you, making it a double tragedy!

We are quite unaware why such events happen!
Destiny always manages to hide the reasons!
But your life does extol an eternal fact Ahilan!
Your passing does prove, that the writer's pen
is indeed a much mightier power, than the gun
though journalists still continue to be prime targets!
Your father's caustic pen earned him lots of enemies
who wanted to silence him. They imprisoned him,
then blasted his press, and when he managed to
escape their attempt, they punished him and your
teacher mother forever by cruelly extinguishing you,
the one and only shining light of their lives!

Violence and crime are never solutions Ahilan,
and any performance is always heightened
by challenge! Others may have fallen,
but your father has succeeded to pave
his own path of excellence, winning acclaim
and accord by his diverse services in Canada,
and his pen continues to command, stronger than ever!

16. THE CLOSED DOOR

Oh! The healing balm that is this immortal
Mozart symphony! How welcome is the
haunting melody as it envelops, lulls
and soothes my turbulent mind.
Assuaged, my memory flits
back to that high watermark
of the ever-flowing tide of my life . . .

It was in 1964, that we two tea-planter couples,
young Sri Lankans, Tamil and Sinhalese,
Lalitha , Rajah Brodie, Srini and Jagathsena
enjoyed four months furlough leave abroad
touring UK and the vast continent
cocooned together in a speeding self drive car
exhilarated, wide-eyed with wonder
imbibing all the various sights, sounds and smells.

The spicy roadside rice and curry meals
hat Srini and I managed to cook on two tiny
spirit stoves with our limited foreign exchange.
Rice, meat, lentils, tinned and dried fish,
while Jagathsena and Rajah washed up
in the clear cold streams and roadside taps
camping and even sharing rooms in pensionnes . . .

My first sight and taste of devilled octopus
and pizza, then available only in Italy.

A slim thirty-year-old mother of five was I
then enjoying this holiday, when with longing
I threw that lucky coin over my shoulder
into The Fountain of Trevi, with it's beautiful
sculpture and blue fountain, making the wish
that I would return to ravishing Rome once again.
That marvellous city of contrasts, the old
and the new, the maddening traffic,
blaring horns, jostling crowds. The galleries
of ancient sculpture and painting
The Vatican, St.Pauls, the Sistine chapel
immortalizing the genius of Michael Angelo.
Pilgrim's requests to pose beside our sarees!
The holidaymakers thronging the beaches
skirting the warm blue Italian sea . . .

We two couples, Tamil and Sinhalese
shared every expense and experience
and got on so well, that there was not even one
small misunderstanding to mar our relationship.
We really did have a good time together.

But now, how radically has the time changed!
The destructive devil that is war, ravages

our beloved motherland, dividing us into two
fighting factions destroying, killing each other
with the never ending thirst for vengeance . . .

Sinhalese and Tamil, separated by the closed door
that is the absence of trust, mutual respect,
empathy, two way communication and
understanding the essential needs of each other
which fan the flames of anger and hatred
blinding each to see only the fault of the other
while remaining unaware of their own mistakes . . .

We certainly have to win our independence!
After trying all other non-violent means
we now have no other option, but to fight!
Our boys and girls unselfishly sacrifice their all
and have shown their calibre to the world,
but the unabated carnage still continues!
The State of Sri Lanka simply refuses
to recognize even our basic human needs
and effectively manages to hide the true picture
from the world with strict media censorship.
Isn't it time now to try to end this deadlock?
Why not seek international mediation,
and consider other ways and means too
to open this locked door and make a positive
effort to find an acceptable solution to end
the misery that is this war and destruction?

17. MARTYRS' DAY

At this threshold
of the millennium,
thirty thousand of us
Canadian Tamils,
did converge thrice
in ardent batches
on Nov.27, 1999
at CNE Exhibition place,
crowding downtown
and creating history,
as our beloved Toronto
watched wide eyed
with amazed wonder!

With heavy hearts
and tear rimmed eyes
did we gather together,
to pay homage, salute,
honour and remember
our immortal heroes!

The young martyrs,
both boys and girls
who, of their own accord
chose to sacrifice their all
for the cause of Tamil Eelam!
For the past two decades
these selfless youngsters,
numbering well over 15 000,
each single one of them
with the same feelings
desires and aspirations
as any youth on earth,
under Prabakaran's leadership
rose against the unjust lot
thrust on us Sri Lankan Tamils
by the ruthless Sinhalese rule.

After first resorting to all
non-violent ways and means
of protests and processions,
negotiations and cease fires,
and even fasts unto death,
these valiant warriors,
flocked together with one aim,
forgetting the self, family, friend,
hope, home, comfort,
till they fell one by one!

The world has to understand
that they were literally forced
to tread the path of violence,
by the unjust rule
of the despotic state!

We are well aware
how our community
time and time again
has lost progress
in every possible sphere
due to the discord, divisions
and petty rivalry,
which disrupt harmony
in the eternal wrangle
for control and power.
But this Martyrs' Day
Tamil immigrants worldwide
did accomplish the impossible
to blaze a confident confirmation
of our strength and solidarity!
Tamils, young and old
and even the tottering infirm
assembled to pledge total support
to our victorious leader Praba!
We must always remember
that our unity is our strength!

Let us celebrate this unity
as our spirits soar in joyous flight!
At last our freedom is in sight!
Strict Sri Lankan mass-media
censorship repeatedly distorts
and paints quite a different story!
The people of the world believe it
and carry on regardless
unaware of the pathetic plight
of our suffering civilian brethren.

Oh! World Tamil immigrants
safe in all possible nooks
and corners of the globe!
We fled like shameless cowards
to escape the terror, trauma
and carnage that is this war
which still rages unabated
causing untold destruction
wreck and ruin to our people!
Come one and all! Let us now
unite to help the thousands
of our scattered suffering refugees
suffering without the basic essentials
of food shelter and clothing.
Let each immigrant family
adopt a needy child from our land

for just twenty dollars a month
as a step towards rehabilitation!

Righteousness will always prevail!
Our brave young warriors
move forward like whirlwinds,
reaping the rewards of their toil!
The vanquished Sri Lankan army
is retreating and running away!
Our independence is at last
in sight in the horizon!

Peace is in the air everywhere
and there is celebration and joy
with resolving age old conflicts.
We too want the healing balm of Peace,
PEACE WITH JUSTICE!
Oh You! The United Nations!
The Leaders of the world!!
The International Mass Media!
Please hasten and come forward
at least now, even at this stage
to intervene and initiate
all what is essential
to negotiate for harmony
and a JUST PEACE,
for us to forge forward

with freedom and joy
to greet the new millennium!

18. CANADA DAY
1.7.2002

Happy Birthday! Happy 135th Birthday, O Canada!
We, members of The Senior Tamil Center, Ontario,
gather to greet you today with boundless love
and joy. Our voices rise together to praise you
with a brimming heart as our gratitude gushes forth
like the cascading Niagara, for what you have
already done and yet continue to do for us.
When we had to flee our war-ravaged homeland,
you magnanimously opened your doors wide to
welcome, grant refuge, shelter and offer a brand
new life for all of us, numbering well over
three hundred thousand now.

Our habitually hard working hands and sharp minds
keep busy as ever here too, as we slowly blend in to
enrich the vast, vibrant mosaic of your multicultural
mainstream. We are proud of all our achievements
in your bosom so far and we assure you, we'll

continue to endeavour with all our might to bedeck
and adorn you with more and more dazzling
jewels of our skilled enterprise and expertise in
every known and possible field.

The dove of Peace hovers ever so slowly over
our homeland now and we await its descent with
abated breath and expectant hearts. Air-flights are
now daily packed as our people flock to Tamil
Eelam to visit precious relatives, well loved
homes, and habitual haunts . . .

Oh! How I long to step on the soil of my beloved
Tamil Eelam, the land of my birth, joyful
childhood and youth, once again!
Oh! To breathe the air of freedom, to taste
the food, the fish and the fruit, the mouth watering
kool, karuvadu, karuppani rice, kurakkan pittu,
the delectable illuppai-poo urundai, ural-pounded
manioc and sambol, the special mutton and
delicious sea food from the Columbuthurai lagoon . .

I visualize with nostalgia, the pervading piety in our
St.Anthonys' church!
How lovely it will be to worship Nallur Kanthan
at His annual chariot festival, as bakthas' devotion,

75

kavadi dancers and bhajans sanctify the surroundings!
Our patient wait outside, awaiting the appearance
of the adorned deities, borne aloft on the bare
shirtless shoulders of eager young men, while flaming
camphor and broken coconuts signify vanishing egos.
Our joy in joining to pull the bedecked chariot
around the temple, the carnival atmosphere,
the rows of hundreds of small make-shift shops,
the jostling crowds, the shopping spree and the busy
bargaining battle all of us indulge in during the
latter part of the twenty-five day festivals.
Our trek back home amidst chatter and laughter,
crunching fresh roasted hot corn, kadalai and peanuts!

It is lovely to be back from Eelam in time for this
celebration today!
It is indeed great that Canada has gifted us
so much, to raise our standard of living.
What can we give in return to show gratitude to our
gracious benefactor?
We can sure contribute a lot so that we leave
not only Canada but the world too a better place!

Why not first lobby for nominated Tamil MP's,
to voice our concerns and needs, as we are
scattered and cannot elect our own community

representatives to the Canadian parliament?
It's a pity that abuse and violence stealthily
stalk almost every community and the mass-media
daily abounds with reports of the worst aspects of
humanity! Seniors, so respected back at home,
are crushed by the reversal of status here,
the taunts of children and even grandchildren
amidst the generation gap, relationship conflicts,
climatic and lifestyle changes, the denial of
qualifications, expertise and experience, the
language barrier, transportation and mobility,
living space, privacy, isolation/loneliness,
awareness/access to adequate home-care
and to available Legal Aid, plus hiding the
trauma of female menopause and male andropause,
without accepting the transience of this physical
sheath, which is the cause of all problems
which hinder graceful aging and spirituality.

What can and what should every one of us do
to stem this downward trend?
We have just this one chance to live!
Let us utilize all our faculties to the utmost,
Practice the Human Values of Love, Truth,
Right-conduct, Peace and Non-violence
and daily nurture our personal growth, to realize

our full potential as human beings.
O come! Let everyone of us make resolve today
to strengthen in balanced manner, not only
our body and mind, but the pining spirit too,
so that our self-esteem will soar and the need
for violence to exert power and control
to bolster our ego disappears for good.
We must realize that we are actually
spiritual beings in a physical experience!
We neither bring or take anything with us
and must not lead too materialistic lives.

**The best recipe for prevention and eradication
of all negativity in the world today is boosting
Individual Personal Growth, which will ensure
Happy Families, Healthy Communities
Harmonious Nations and Universal Spirituality
culminating in a Vibrant
Humanity.**

19. WAR AND PEACE
JANUARY 2003

From time immemorial
it is certainly true that
War and Peace
have been entwined
along with our entrails
inside every one of us.
We've always tried
with all our might
to assert our power
and control over
the significant other
in our environment.
We have also learnt to nurture
only our transient body
and the fickle mind, utterly
neglecting our eternal spirit.

However, this unhealthy trend
seems to be definitely changing
with the present steady spread of
spiritual awareness and awakening,
slowly changing attitudes
and actions of people everywhere.

The mass-media now extols
the absolute need for reflection,
self-analysis and self-correction
to speed personal growth
and raise self-esteem, along with
the observance of the eternal
human values of Love, Truth,
Right conduct, Non-violence
and Forgiveness for Peace and Joy.

Bang! Bang! that unprecedented 911
terrorist destruction of the twin towers
of New York in 2001, was indeed a shocking
and heart wrenching surprise to every one of us!
However, what has been the repercussion?
Instead of strict self analysis/self criticism
to determine and totally eliminate
the real reasons and mistakes that must
have definitely instigated this calculated
and well planned terrorist attack,
isn't it sad that the mighty USA,
the leading power of the world,
is so negatively bent on wreaking
revenge, by starting World War 3?

We, The Voice of Women for Peace
along with ten thousand women and men

in Toronto, of every age, creed and color,
braved the bitter weather and joined
others from every nation in Global Harmony,
to march with saucy slogans and
fiery placards, vehemently protesting against
the proposed USA attack on Iraq!
Will you, American President Bush
please listen to us and stop your attack?
None of us want war! Especially we
Sri Lankans, definitely do not want war!
War is so easy to start but so difficult to stop!
We have experienced it and personally
know the absolute terror, destruction,
annihilation and utter loss that is war!

At last the dove of peace now hovers
ever so slowly over our motherland
Sri Lanka and we eagerly await its descent
with abated breath and expectant hearts.
Please, please do listen to our voices!
If you listen, Saddam will listen to us too!
Nobody ever wins in a war! So stop it!
Let us all unite to create a world filled with
Love, Truth, Non-violence, Peace and Joy.

Published By Voice Of Women For Peace Canada

LONDON BOMBS
7.7.2005

Early morning today, four suicide bomb blasts
in three subway trains and a bus, jolted Tony Blair,
London and the world into shocked awareness
of the urgent need for change in UK foreign policies!
Similar to the 2400 Madrid pre-election bomb blasts
in March 2004, a new Al Qaeda breed of locally born
and bred Muslim fanatics have simultaneously struck
to proclaim their existence, anger, hatred and power!
Over fifty commuters died, hundreds wounded,
while the whole world watches without knowing
what exactly has to be done to stem this carnage
and prevent similar suicide attacks in the future!

Isn't it a real coincidence that I was in London
during 911 in 2001, and I am here this time too?
The Madrid bombs did help to change the course
of Spanish elections! I suppose this new breed
of London suicide bombers seek change too!
Terrorists try it again on the 21st Thursday also
but the four bombs fail to detonate and they are
arrested! However, what an inhuman method to
seek change! Why choose suicide bombs, the

worst possible way to request change! Should so
many precious lives
be lost and so much of innocent blood be shed,
all because fanatics feel that change is essential?
Surely, in this 21st century, aren't there better ways
and means to get the message across and achieve
results?

20. HINDU NEW YEAR SUBANU
14.4.2003

Welcome! Welcome, new year Subanu 2003!
No doubt, your name itself portends good luck!
Now that the three week battle of Baghdad is over
and there is no war anywhere else too,
your dawn does at last herald world peace!
Amidst New Year festivities, with immense relief
at the termination of civilian casualties, I do hope
that global Peace with Justice will now prevail.

The current, opulent world mass-media coverage
of the US invasion of Iraq makes my mind reel
and flit back to compare it with the scant reports
of our trials, tribulations and losses in the twenty

year ethnic conflict in my motherland Sri Lanka.
That tyrant war, wears so many different masks
in the quest to fulfil his lust for power and control!
We too welcomed the Indian Peace Keeping Force
with hope in 1989, trusting that peace would be
restored, but unfortunately strive escalated instead.

Thousands of us were forced to vacate our homes
and bunkers to seek refuge in bold roof identified
over-crowded temples, churches and schools,
sans electricity, running water, sanitation, food or
Medi-care. Aerial bombs, mortars, shells and
gunfire pounded us continually, claiming so many
innocent civilian lives, while the only hospital
struggled to cope with the wounded. The well
marked UNHCR and Red Cross quarters were
not spared either and came under severe attack too!
Our shops and offices were looted like in Baghdad.
Houses were swept clean of even doors, windows
plus roof tiles! The army killed, raped, tortured,
looted and bulldozed houses at their whim
and fancy! There was no one to check or stop
them and with strict censorship, this side
of the story was never relayed to the world,
and it is history that no super-power
intervened to help us in our hour of need.

It is great that at last the peace process in Sri Lanka
was initiated an year ago, but it is progressing
ever so slowly, while Tamils from far and wide,
flock home now to visit kith and kin and try
to remember the old faces of favourite haunts,
so wantonly destroyed and changed by the war.
Oh! I have seen more than enough of the terror
that is war and I mourn for all lost lives
in every single war and persecution!
We have launched so many space ships,
satellites and such. Why can't we find a solution
to prevent war forever in the future?
Temples, churches, schools, libraries, hospitals
and houses can be re-built and no doubt that unlike
poor struggling Sri Lanka,
oil rich Iraq will be
restored rapidly by
international coalition.
But who will answer
for the irreplaceable lives
of lost loved ones?

Lalitha

21. 'PONGU THAMIL'
SOLIDARITY & CELEBRATION
OF TAMILS - 25.9.2004

We Tamils from Thamil Eelam, young, old and even
the tottering infirm have converged today
in hitherto unprecedented numbers
creating history and crowding Queens Park
led by the Canadian Tamil Students, in the wake
of The Students of Thamil Eelam
while beloved Toronto and the world
watch wide eyed with wonder and amazement.

Yes! The world is aware how our community
time and time again, has lost vim and vigor and
progress due to our discord and divisions in every
possible sphere plus petty rivalry, which disrupts
harmony in the eternal wrangle for power and
control. But that is all past and today
on our first observance of 'Pongu Thamil',
we have gathered to pledge total support to
celebrate our unity under the banner of our able
leader Prabaharan and proclaim to the world our
solidarity with elation!

We Tamils are essentially industrious and peace
loving. We were literally forced to rise in protest
against the injustices and atrocities thrust on us by
the state, resulting in the internal war that has
relentlessly heaped heartbreaking losses,
suffering and destruction in Sri Lanka.
We Canadian Tamil immigrants, well over three
hundred thousand now and others spread far and
 wide, safe in all possible nooks and corners of the
 globe, fled our beloved motherland to escape the
 terror and   trauma that is this war, wreaking wreck
 and ruin to our people.

Though Peace Negotiations began over two years
ago, the dove of peace seems reluctant to alight in
Sri Lanka! We are tired of waiting for its descent.
It is true that there is no war now, but neither
have we peace and there is no progress in sight!
Most of our people still suffer as homeless refugees
without a definite, permanent settlement.
We wish to end this stalemate and now seek
only for an acceptable interim accord
but the state insists on a permanent solution!
WE WANT PEACE! PEACE WITH JUSTICE!
We want to re-start the Peace Negotiation

which has so unfortunately come to a standstill
now in-spite of Norwegian mediation.
The Sri Lankan Govt. seems to be not interested
in genuinely nurturing the Peace process anymore.

We are here today to join and raise our voices together!
We yearn for freedom to enjoy our basic human rights!
Oh! You The United Nations! The Leaders of the
world! You The Mighty Mass Media and The
Internet! You, our dearly beloved benefactor Canada!
We cry out once again and appeal to you all for help!
Will you please, please do at least now intervene
to ensure that the now faltering Peace Process in
Sri Lanka is appropriately tended and nurtured with
care and concern so that PEACE WITH JUSTICE
is restored to us, and to every other country caught
in the coils of continuous war too, to usher in
a golden new era of global peace and prosperity.

22.   JAFFNA   2004

I am so happy that I am on this treasured trip
to Jaffna at last, after the long twelve year wait!
I choose the night bus and try to sleep,

but the bumpy ride makes me sore as ever.
Long stops at several army check points
delay us a lot and I eagerly await the dawn.

The dry terrain is very much the same as we drive
past and there are no signs at all of any progress.
The division of Tamil Eelam starts at Omanthai
and from then on we pass bomb/shell-scarred buildings.
Murugandy Temple is the same but the surroundings
look different. At Nanthavanam we get the
Eelam passports from the LTTE check point.
We arrive tired at cousin Praba Kamalanathan's
for a tasty late lunch. Relations and friends pour in.
It is so good to be with them all, once again.

I have just three days in Jaffna before leaving for
Australia. I hire an Auto for the day and visit everyone.
Ammah's sister Mahes Ammah looks alright at 89
and it is lovely to spend time with her. I miss Sithappah
a lot and feel so sad that I didn't come to see him
before his fatal accident. All the kids have grown
up such a lot and I hardly recognize them.

I visit our two houses which are rented out.
I am surprised that though we built and cared
so much for them earlier, I have no feelings

at all for them now! A house is really not a home!
It is people and relationships that make it a home!
Only the bare walls remain in Ravi/Nalayini's
new house as all valuables, doors, windows,
and even roof tiles/timber have been stolen!

It is great to see the new face of Chundikuli Girl's
College and I could just feel the vibrations of its
progress! The Jaipur Artificial Foot Workshop too
has expanded and I manage to find a known face or
two amongstall the new comers. It is lovely to meet
two of the Founder member Lady Doctors,
Physician Dr.Mrs.Ganesamoorthy and
Dr.Mrs.Theivendram who unlike many,
chose to stay on in the war zone to continue
their selfless service. I visit Shanthiyaham
where a training session was in progress.
It is so good to see friends Stephen, Shiromi
and kids coming up again after all their losses.
I manage to meet Dr.Daya Somasunderam
for a few minutes, rendering yeoman service
at the Psychiatric ward of the Jaffna hospital.
It is so heart-warming to meet caring Father
Rev.Damian, visit his new Holistic Health Centre
on Vembadi Rd. providing much needed care

and help for the welfare of afflicted single
women and children, with help from UNICEF.

Main Street in Jaffna town is covered with weeds
and looks dilapidated. However, the Nallur Temple
is being renovated and the 'Archanai' ticket is still
only a rupee! Time flies on swift wings and it is
soon time for me to depart. I leave by plane
to Colombo with a heavy heart. I am not sure
when I will visit beloved Jaffna again!

23. THE DAWN OF THAMIL EELAM

We are at a critical point in our history of Thamil Eelam now! Will you open your visionary eye and join me please?

Do you hear those loud cheers of joyous jubilation? The music of 'conches, 'nadaswarams' and drums of celebration? Yes! Thamil Eelam has dawned, really dawned at last! After all the struggles, setbacks and losses we have won our freedom! Come on! Let us participate and enjoy this momentous event!

Some sing, some dance and everyone is so full of joy! After hoisting our Tiger Flag, receiving honour and adulation, inspecting the Guard of Honour and the March Past our beloved leader Prabaharan, who led us to this victory, bows his head with tear rimmed eyes, to remember with gratitude, revere and pay homage and opens the curtain of the giant granite edifice, that will eternally honour our Martyrs, both girls and boys, numbering well over 18000.

These valiant young 'MaVeerars' including Black Tigers, sacrificed their all, unselfishly for the cause of Thamil Eelam, and we too join our leader in silence with reverence.

Praba continues and pays homage to all the civilians who lost their lives in the twenty-year internal war. He thanks all the soldiers maimed and crippled in the struggle, and praises the parents who sent their children so willingly to fight for the cause. Lifting his head high, he vows with great emotion to lead Thamil Eelam into a golden era of Peace and Prosperity, which generates tremendous applause from the crowd!

The cultural items begin now and the lovely dancers all dressed up arrive, accompanied by the soul-stirring singers. The dancers sway in rhythm to the heart rending sad music, to pay homage and extol the heroism of our fallen heroes. Every single name of our martyrs will as a jewel adorn each and every new building sprouting in Tamil Eelam! The massive skyscrapers, the ultra modern hospitals, The Trincomalee Harbour, The main Vanni Secretariat, The Palali International Airport, The wide multiple lane Highways, The Subway Train Station Network, The Main Jaffna University trailed by Colleges and Schools, Temples, Churches, Mosques, Libraries, Art galleries, Arts & Crafts, Gymnasiums, Museums, Tourist attractions, Seaside Resorts and Hotels, Counseling Centres, Theatres, Underground Housing Complexes, Free Trade Zones, Shopping Centres, and Industrial Factories etc.

Now the music turns jubilant and the dancers
twist and twirl around to the joyous rhythm
expressing their pride and joy! "We now have our
freedom! We will forget all our differences and petty
rivalry for control and power. We will not make
mistakes again! Let us unite to nurture the progress of
Thamil Eelam! This is our one and only goal and priority
now! We will focus not only on material but spiritual
growth too. Education in Human values will be
compulsory in our schools. We will nurture not only
our Tamil language and culture to reach lofty heights,
but the world language English too. The degrading
caste system decreed by ancient Manu which we so
blindly followed without question earlier, will be
abolished from Thamil Eelam for good! The terrible
dowry system, which enslaved us, will vanish too.

Thamil Eelam may be impoverished geographically
with no rivers and scanty rainfall, but we are rich
in human resources. Our Tamil maestros in every
field around the globe will surge into our land
to elevate our standard of life. Industrialists will exploit
our natural resources of sea-food, fresh flowers,
and fruit, mango, jak other fruits and vegetables.
Our palmyra fruit juice, jam, jaggery, treacle,
'pannatu', 'pulukkodial' and 'odial' will become

famous in the world. Our seafood specials,
cultured prawns and canned squid eggs
will vie with Russian caviar and definitely win
the world market. Hot hoppers, thosai and other
 food items delivered pizza style, will be the talk
of the town! Our Precious gems, cultured pearls
and handcrafted gold jewellery will be the fashion
rage amongst the richest women of the world!

It is now time for us to show our true colours!
Haven't we wasted all this time from ancient days
without any visible achievement whatsoever?
The Chinese built the great Wall long ago!
The Egyptians can still boast of the ancient
pyramids, to prove their enterprise and skill.
The North Indians have the Taj Mahal.
How is it that we Tamils, especially Sri Lankans,
have nothing wonderful to feel proud of?
We took it too easy, never took any risks
or cultivated different lines of thought.
We became addicted to the security of pensions
doled out by the English Govt. to enslave us!
We are notorious for patting our own backs
and exchanging garlands only among ourselves!
Let us stop singing our past glories at least now!
Let us tarry no longer! Come on! Start the action!

Our nation has arrived at last and it is now time
to prove that we are equal to the best in the whole world!
Our real strength is our intelligent human resources!
Our scientists will exploit solar power, wind-power,
bio-gas, fresh water from the sea, underground irrigation
and artificial rain too, to cultivate around the year.
With our energetic enterprise we will prove to everyone
that we are second to none! Let us chisel the name
of our Thamil Eelam in golden letters in world history!

III. GENERAL

24. THAI PONGAL - HINDU FESTIVAL OF THANKSGIVING

Its Thaipongal time in the nineteen-forties in Jaffna!
Appah has come on leave from Colombo
to celebrate this annual Hindu festival of thanksgiving.
I join appah in a crowded bus ride to Jaffna town
the previous day, to do the pongal shopping.
How very true it is, that the joy of any festival
begins with the purchase of the essentials
for its celebration! We carefully select the new
earthenware pot, (It is a bad omen if a pongal pot
leaks or breaks during pongal!) with the ginger
and saffron leaves to tie round adorning its neck,
(Metal pots are used now) along with betel leaves,
arecanuts, three different varieties of bananas,
mangoes, sugar cane, jaggery, raisens, cadju nuts,
camphor, fire crackers and a host of other things.

We rise early on pongal morn, bathe, wear new clothes
and start helping appah and ammah with the chores.
Ammah cleans and prepares the courtyard in front
of our house and papa decorates and draws an artistic
'kolam' pattern on the cow-dunged ground with

white flour (food for the ants!)with gaps on all four
sides so that the Sun can enter to partake of the feast!
The pot full of water 'Nirai-kudam' with its
crown of mango leaves and coconut,
regally sits on its plantain leaf and paddy
padded throne. A coconut is broken to signify
the breakdown of our egos. The pongal pot filled
to the brim with water and milk, is set on top
of three fire bricks by appah and we start stoking
the fire with coconut fronds. The fire burns bright
and quick, the milk rises, forms a white crown on top
of the pot which tilts and flows out in the direction
of the rising sun, now shining bright happily
accepting our offering. Firecrackers are lit
announcing the success our of pongal to neighbours.

Appah adds three handfuls of rice and lentils into the
boiling pot and we all follow suit with our handfuls
of rice. While the rice simmers ammah gets the
coconut milk and jaggery solution ready while
we chop the cadju nuts. The mixed vegetable
sambar curry is also bubbling by the side of the
pongal pot. When the rice is done ammah
adds the sweetened coconut milk, powdered

cardamoms, cloves, cinnamon and last of all
the ghee roasted nuts and raisens.
The aroma of the delicious pongal rice
fills the air, as we arrange banana leaves
on the ground and light the ceremonial oil lamps.
We serve the pongal and sweetmeats on banana leaves
placed on the ground, worship God, sing
devotional hymns and offer our gratitude to the sun.

You must eat it to realise how divine the combination
of the sweet rice and the spicy curries taste!
We worship at the temple too and visit friends
and relations to mutually exchange sweetmeats.
We participate in the village sports meet
in the afternoon and enjoy the treat of a lovely
cultural presentation by village maestros at night.

Though Hindus scattered in every part of the globe
may not be able to make the traditional pongal offering
to the sun in the courtyard in front of their houses,
every Hindu will definitely observe this ceremony
and offer thanks in a temple or inside their homes.

25. THE STORY OF BHEESHMAR
From The Mahabharatha

I am sure that most of you know that the ancient Mahabharatha is one of the greatest epics in the multilingual literature of the world. I give below the unusual story of selfless Bheeshmar, from the Mahabharatha.

It is a lovely evening. As the young fishermen set out to sea, the young maidens revel in dance and song along with Sathiawathy, the beautiful adopted daughter of the leader of the fisherfolk.

King Santhanu who comes along, is enchanted by Sathiawathy and at once falls in love with her. The king tells her of his love and entreats her to marry him. Sathiawathy replies that she will marry him only with the permission of her father. King Santhanu asks for the father's blessings for this marriage, but the father lays down a condition. He says that the king can marry her, only if he promises that Sathiawathy's son will become king, over-riding the present heir to the throne Thevavirathan known as Kankeyan. The disappointed king Santhanu, unable to grant this request, returns to his palace with sorrow, torn between his consuming passion for Sathiawathy and his love for his eldest son Kankeyan.

When crown prince Kankeyan realizes the reason for the king's depression and sorrow, he meets Sathiawathy's father and makes a vow to convince him that he will forsake the throne and be a bachelor for life. The father then agrees for the marriage happily. Kankeyan takes Sathyawathy to the palace in his chariot.

King Santhanu is first very upset that his son Kankeyan has renounced the throne and taken the vow of celibacy, but recovers and marries Sathiawathy. He blesses Kankeyan and confers on him the highest honour of Bheeshmar and also grants him the boon to choose the manner of his death.

Time never tarries and twenty years whiz past! When king Santhanu dies, Sathiawathy entreats Bheeshmar to forget his promise of celibacy 'bramacharya' and become king. Bheeshmar declines the offer and is adamant that he will crown Sathyawathy's son Visithiraveeryan as king. Bheeshmar insists that before the coronation, Visithraveeriyan should attend the 'Suyamvara' ceremony of the daughters of the king of

Kasi where the three princesses would choose their husbands.

The attendants escort the three princesses of Kasi, Ambai, Ambikai and Ambalikai to the Suyamvara chamber where all the eligible princes are assembled. While introducing the princes, the attendants make fun of the aged prince Bheeshmar, who gets angry and challenges all the young princes to combat. He fights and defeats every single prince, and takes his brother Visithiraveeryan and the three princesses to Hasthinapuram.

Bheeshmar begins the arrangements for the wedding of his brother Visithiraveeryan to the three princesses. But princess Ambai discloses that she is in love with the vanquished Prince Chaluvan, wishes to marry him and asks for Bheeshmar's help. Bheeshmar understands her plight and sends her over to prince Chaluvan. Princess Ambai goes to prince Chaluvan who says, "How can I accept you, after you were taken by another prince in his chariot?" and refuses to accept Ambai.

Disappointed princess Ambai returns to Hasthinapuram and pleads with Visithiraveeryan to accept her.

Visithraveeryan spurns her saying,
"I cannot marry you as you were in love
with someone else". Desperate Ambai begs
Bheeshmar to marry her. But he replies,
"I am sorry but I cannot marry you as I observe
bramacharya. Do not insult me like this. Please
go away". Enraged Ambai, vows to wreak
vengeance on Bheeshmar and runs away.

Ambai goes to guru Parasuramar and relates
her sad story to him. Incensed Parasuramar
fights with Bheeshmar, but is defeated in battle.

Exasperated Ambai turns to Lord Muruga,
pours out her heart and worships him with penance.
Pleased with her piety, Lord Murugan grants
her a garland of lotus flowers which will
never fade and says that only the person who
wears that garland can kill Bheeshmar.
Ambai gives thanks to the deity and leaves,
determined to somehow kill Bheeshmar.

To Ambai's dismay all are mortally scared,
and nobody ventures to wear the garland
and kill Bheeshmar. Disillusioned, Ambai
turns to Lord Siva and performs austere thapas.

Lord Siva , utterly pleased appears
before her and says, "There is nobody
living on earth now, who can kill Bheeshmar.
May you be reborn again, and kill Bheeshmar",
and Ambai commits suicide.

Ambai is re-born as Chihandy, daughter of King
Thrupatha in her next birth. When she grows up
to be a young maiden, she wears the eternally
fresh garland of lotuses to fulfill her vow to kill
Bheeshmar. Her father is very frightened to offend
Bheeshmar and chases his daughter away from his
kingdom. Chihandy hangs that ever fresh garland of
red lotuses at the doorstep of Thrupathan's palace
and runs away.

There is a festival on the bank of river Ganges
where the celestial Kantharva sage Thumburu, has
to act as a woman in a drama and is searching
for someone to exchange bodies with him.
He asks Chihandy whether she will give him
her female form and take his male form.
Chihandy, who is waiting for an opportunity to kill
Bheeshmar gladly agrees and they exchange bodies.
Chihandy, now a male, wears the garland
of lotuses and sets out to kill Bheeshmar.

It is the tenth day of the great battle between the
cousins, The five Pandavas and hundred The Kauravas
of Mahabharatha. Chihandy in male form, becomes
the charioteer of Arjuna and aims her arrow to kill
Bheeshmar. Bheeshmar, realises through his divine sixth
sense, that the male Thumburu is really the female
Chihandy and wavers for a moment whether he should
aim his arrow at a woman. In that split second,
Arjuna's arrow pierces Bheeshmar's chest,
he falls on his bed of arrows and has a heroic death.

26.   PEACE

The calm blue sea
reflecting the cloudless sky above
meditates wave-less and serene,
undisturbed in the tranquil peace
that emanates from it, which pervades
everything that my eye beholds.
This in turn, sparks my inward eye
to introvert and explore the vast expanse
of my fickle mind, to become aware
of my blind area of faults and frailties . . .

I now realise that I can change only myself
to create an example and tread the middle path
in order to awaken others, to change on their own.
I must first accept and love my very own-self
and continue to mature in personal growth.
I will always endeavour to touch my core inside
communicate my love unconditionally and try to
accept everyone around me exactly as they are . . .
I know how very difficult this is, more easily said
than done. Please grant me the strength
my Lord, to make my musings materialise . . .

The still calm of the blue sea and the sky
now embrace me, infect and instil peace and
tranquillity in my mind too.
How very true it is, that selfless love and peace
must first spring and pour forth from
each and every individual self, spread
into the family, community and the nation
to lay the firm foundation to spread everlasting
peace and joy in the whole wide world!

27. THE OPPOSITES

After the habitual argument
they drove on in solemn, sullen silence
not uttering a word to each other
that whole afternoon, all the way from Colombo!
Five tedious hours! Cocooned in the climbing car
while Pathma pondered and mused
on the inexplicable, intricate web of life,
that arranges and weaves together
the most unlikely opposites
in sacred matrimony for life.

As they approached salubrious Kandy,
horn blaring loud as ever,
a noisy truck overtook them
packed with singing girls!
Teenagers! Twanging two guitars!
Clapping, swaying with mincing steps,
keeping time to the music.
Senior schoolgirls, returning from a picnic!
Oh, You exuberant carefree youth!
Carrying all future dreams in your starry eyes!
Oh! You lovely children!
What sort of marriage will be yours?
1995

28. SOLITUDE

1993

I am all-alone at home today
without any agenda, and it is so quiet.
I drink greedily from this cup of solitude
and it revives and replenishes
my body, mind and soul . . .
I must sit down to write more . . .
Chisel my thoughts into words of song
enhanced and embellished with my etchings
that will conquer the ravages of time
to be immortalized into eternity . . .

I continue to watch my mind
bemused at all its fickle wanderings.
I repeatedly continue making the mistake
of believing that I have my mind in control.
However, this latest desire now consumes me!

29. MY MIND

1993

The mind! The mind! My fickle mind!
I have great fun watching you!
For quite sometime now, I have been aware
of all your restless jumps here and there.
I try to tighten my reins to tame you
However wily you, somehow manage to shake me
off and once again a supreme reign!

2005

My mind! My mind! You have won!
You are the master once again as I cringe in shame,
sadly realizing that I seem to be sliding down!
After my addiction to vegetarianism for the last twenty-
two years, how did you manage to change me
to triumph and win over my aged instincts too?
It all started because my
specialist said that I
(Stingy me!) have to spend
800 dollars a month and
change to new drug Forteo
instead of free Fosmax, as my bone
density is deteriorating fast!

I reflected, "OK! I am hurting myself,
because I abhor hurting other lives!
I will just eat sardines to improve
my bones!" However, that first cutlet
broke all barriers, and from the last X'mas party,
I confess I started to consume non-veg. again!
The surprising twist is that I, who genuinely
hated to even taste meat or fish gravy for salt
and spices earlier, am now enjoying all the
non-vegetarian food so unashamedly!

I now realize that my mind is the culprit!
My natural instinct to be healthy, seems to
have won over all my beliefs and prejudices!
I have stopped wearing my Rudraksha beads!
I am trying hard to console myself that
even great saints like Sri Ramakrishna
and Swami Vivekananda did enjoy eating fish!
I realize the amazing power of the mind more
and more! Brainwashing creates even suicide
bombers! I am aware how absolutely essential it is
to cultivate a well balanced, controlled mind,
so that we become the supreme masters
and not petty slaves of our fickle minds.

30. MOTHER TERESA
1910 – 1997

Beloved Mother Teresa!

Marvellous angel of mercy!

Though you were of Albanian descent

You chose to be domiciled in Calcutta

To lead The Sisters of Charity

With your timeless example

Of selfless empathy, unconditional

Love, compassion and care

To serve the poorest of the poor!

Your saree clad figure, tiny and frail

With face so wrinkled and worn,

Does stand out as a shining saint,

Towering above all others,

As the lady of the century!

31. QUEEN OF HEARTS
1961 – 1997

Beloved Princess Diana
Queen of hearts
And selfless service.
Blessed with
All what humanity
Yearns for in life!
Beauty, name
Power and fame.

You are the ultimate
Example to prove
That contentment and joy
Cannot come from outside
Nor from material wealth
Which palls before the treasure
Of blessed spiritual heights!

32. CENTENARIAN CHUNDIKULI
1996

We give thanks to our Lord
With a grateful heart
For this celebration of the Centenarian
Our Beloved Almamater, Chundikuli

The frail little barque
Launched by early Christian Missionaries
Has weathered many a storm
With the strength and determination
And the splendid selfless service
Of the different crews and captains
Who have led Her to the present pinnacle
of peerless achievement and glory.

Chundikuli girls, hoisting high
Our gleaming banner all Red and Black
Stand out as sturdy shining beacons
in every possible nook and corner
Of the whole wide world today.
Serving humanity with concern and care
Raising the standard of life everywhere.
The Chundikuli girl is the ideal daughter
Sister, wife, mother, grandmother

Mother-in-law, relative friend and neighbour
The best employee and employer
in every single possible profession
and the all-sacrificing freedom seeker.
We hold our heads high, in elation
With love, gratitude and devotion.

Are we wrong to envision our freedom?
But the terror of war now envelops our land
and our cities still shudder under siege.
Well more than a hundred & seventy thousand
of us have fled our beloved Motherland
and sought refuge in this multicultural
hospitable haven that is Canada
where we endeavour to expand our horizons.
'Operation Sunshine' has driven our people away
and alas, Jaffna is now a ghost town!

Chundikuli too, deserted, She stands!
We may now stumble, but we have absolute faith
That the light of dawn is definite after the darkness
God Almighty, one and only, is still in control
and though it is not clear, life does unfold as destined.
Our majestic Chundikuli Eagle will again be in full flight.
Eagerly soaring Forward to explore the potential
of both the unknown cosmos and the human mind.
Come! Let us join together and praise the Lord.

33. MRS.G.E.S.CHELLIAH

Silver haired, serene and smiling she stands
beside her beloved partner, Mr.J.T.Chelliah.
Both mellowed veteran educationists
still vibrant and ramrod straight
eyes aglow with spiritual peace
and the gratification of selfless service
to the lofty giants in Jaffna, Sri Lanka
St. John's and Chundikuli Girls' Colleges.

It was on the ninth of January, nineteen twenty
That Daniel and Harriet Walton were blest
with their first born, Grace Ellen Saraswathy,
followed by three more, Eva, Parames and Mano.
Like the tinkling chimes of bells that herald
the mighty elephant, was it providence
that prompted the proud parents with the foresight
to name her after the Hindu Goddess of wisdom?
For this chosen Christian child would in the future
blossom out with spreading fragrance
into one of our best educationists of all times,
skilfully steering the helm of our dear old school
through turbulent times, with such magnificent success
that proud Chundikuli, now stands out as a lighthouse

attracting, shaping and moulding more and more
women worldwide, who illumine and adorn every
sphere of life.

At the tender age of four, Saras joined the LKG
to be nurtured with the eternal values in Chundikuli
tradition, and forward she marched
with never a look behind.
She passed her Senior Cambridge in
1936, continued her Inter Art and Matric
at Jaffna College and completed
her London BA at the Colombo University.
She taught at The Holy Family Convent, Jaffna
for a while and joined her Almamater
as a teacher in 1945. She imparted her love
of maths and poetry to us, her students, stirring our
creativity by encouraging us
to read our good essays out to class.
She was our Form III class teacher,
a brilliant set including the present principal
Mrs.Pathma Jeyaweerasingam.
She married gentle Mr.J.T.Chelliah in 1948
and they were soon blessed with their only child,
Indranee.

Mrs.Chelliah did her postgraduate
in London and teaching became her vocation.
In 1960, with the abrupt change of Govt. policy,
Chundikuli was floundering as a private
non-fee levying College. No one wanted to accept
responsibility as the Principal, and the yoke fell
on the reluctant shoulders of Mrs.Chelliah.
Though she was already sick with diabetes
from the age of thirty six, her piety, trust
and faith in God gave her the health, strength
and the wisdom and from 1962 she
marched on as captain, with never a look behind.

At first Chundikuli did have its ups and downs
during the early nineteen sixties. She joined teachers
and trudged from door to door soliciting aid from parents
to run the school. She then met the best and worst
of human nature, but she always emerged victorious,
tirelessly using her full potential of spirit, mind, body
and emotions. She always felt the guiding hand of God
on her shoulder in answer to her prayers. A gale
brought down some classrooms one night, but she
managed to raise enough to build elsewhere, thus
unexpectedly creating quite by chance, a much needed
new track and field to conduct the annual Sports Meets

on home grounds. Chundikuli produced Her best plays
and ballets in both languages during these days.
Many a time the Chelliahs had to transport
the teachers home after play practices at midnight.
Gradually help started pouring in from diverse sources,
The World Council of Curches, The CCF and others.
Chundikuli had at last weathered the storm
and started still continuing her prolific growth.

Mrs.Chelliah is a total product and is literally pickled
in Chundikuli with her association of over seventy
years. Mr.Chelliah, the perfect partner held the
ladder firmly as she climbed higher and higher.
Both of them worked very hard, forgetting personal
comforts and depriving Indranee of parental care.
When there is genuine dedication and sincerity of
service, God works miracles and this happened
now. A golden era of wondrous changes dawned.
Mrs.Chelliah, gentle and unassuming, blossomed
into a great administrator, prolific builder and
adorned everything she touched with her mark of
excellence. Her splendid building spree began with
the construction of the Principal's bungalow, which
had to be tucked away in a corner to make room
for the impressive Jubilee building,

the Administrative block, the well equipped library, and the Science Labs for each of the sciences. She remodelled the old school hall by turning it around and started building towards the sky with three storied class rooms.

The new Kindergarten block, the expanded playground the Thilliyampalam Institute Building and Teachers Quarters with separate entrances sprouted giving a brand new look to Chundikuli!

Mrs.Chelliah retired in 1983 but still continues as the Patron of OGA both in Sri Lanka and Canada.

In time, daughter Indranee married Charles Navaratnarajah and the Chelliahs had the joy of two grandchildren, Jennifer and Denuja whom they grand-parented in Jaffna, while the parents sought greener pastures in Canada. They brought their grandchildren to Toronto in 1987 and turned another new page adapting and coping with an entirely new way of life in a foreign country. they now live in an apartment adjoining Parkwoods Village Church and it is interesting that both who never cooked earlier, are now excellent cooks!

As veteran Patrons of The St.Johns' Chundikuli
Old Students Association, they continue their yeoman
service, organizing events, raising funds and continue
to cement the students of the twin Colleges is service
and fellowship.

It was lovely to meet them when I arrived in
Canada in February 1992. I had the honour of
working with Mr and Mrs. Chelliah in the
committees of The Old Pupil's Associations both in
Jaffna and Canada. Surprisingly we are now batch-
mates in Counselor Trainer Indranee Abeyesekera's
classes in Personal Growth, Understanding
the Enneagram and The Senior Tamil Center
Creative Writing classes! Our Canadian lecturer
wants us to call each other by first names, but my
admiration and respect makes me to still call them
Mr and Mrs.Chelliah!

The world is always full of so many people,
who just live and wither off unknown.
Just a handful get to do what they like,
do their utmost, realise their full potential
and leave their footprints on the sands of time.
Mr. and Mrs.Chelliah are two of the
chosen few, who have entwined their entire life

around their Almamaters enriching
everyone they came in contact with. No doubt
they are human and would have definitely
made mistakes, but the growing faces of both St.Johns'
and Chundikuli bear eloquent testimony to their
selfless service. Their names will live and last
forever in the annals of St.Johns and Chundikuli.
P.S. Mr.J.T.Chelliah 17.9.1915 – 25.4.2005

34. THE CONQUEST OF MARS
JULY 7, 1997

The unmanned American Pathfinder
Speeding across 150 000 00 km. for seven months
has landed on our neighbour in the constellation!
The excellent spaceship kept up to schedule
and has conquered the fiery planet of Mars.
All humanity is agog with jubilation
and space scientists bristle with anticipation.

Deemed first as the Lord of agriculture
and later as the Lord of War by the ancients
Because of its fiery red colour, is the planet Mars.
Predicted by Hindu astrologers as a malefic planet, if
it predominates the seventh, the house of marriage.

122

Man made history and landed on the moon in 1963,
but has anything noteworthy happened after that?
However, the focus of humanity has now
invaded the privacy of the angry red planet!

There is so much that needs to be done
for the welfare of life on our own planet.
Exploration and change are no doubt essentials
for any growth and progress in life.
However please do pause a minute to consider.
Is it fair to spend so much of time, effort and money
to over emphasise the exploration of outer space?
Why not spend even a little, to teach introversion
to explore the vast universe
of the human mind?

35. THE TEA PLUCKER
Demodera Group-1960

The early dawn gong, awakens young Meenatchi from her mat in her one roomed house, sandwiched between the row of line rooms. (These line-rooms were custom-built for Indian Tamil labour, recruited by the earlier British planters, though now some estates provide small cottages). Her stalwart husband Ramu and three kids are still fast asleep on the floor when she finishes her cooking, making the daily menu of rotti, on the open fireplace on a platform in a corner. She wakes them up with tumblers of steaming tea, before rushing out pell-mell with her plucking basket, for the 6 am muster roll call by the strict KG*and conductor.

Her trained hands quickly start plucking and tossing the tender green tea leaves, two leaves and a bud over her shoulder into the large basket on her back. Ramu follows her out for his pruning job task, after leaving the younger kids at the estate day-care creche. The eldest gets ready to attend grade 5 at the estate school managed by two teachers. However, she will have to stop school next year as the Govt. school at Hali-Ela on the main Badulla Rd. is far away and no buses ply on estate roads!

Meenatchi eats her rotti at lunch break, and rain or shine continues briskly, as payment is by weight of green-leaf brought in by each plucker. She starts cooking rice, dried fish and a vegetable curry when she gets home, has a bath, washes clothes and cleans up. They listen to the radio as they have dinner, and join neighbours for the poojah at the estate temple or have a chat before retiring early to bed.

There are two tea factories, a hospital with a doctor plus five Dispensaries on Demodera with its large labour population. Family disputes are taken to the five divisional offices on labour day, to the powerful managers whose word is law!

*KG – Kangany (Supervisor)

36. THE DEMODERA MANJARI (DIGEST)

1963

Powerful Thondaman, leader of The CWC- Ceylon Workers' Congress ensures that all Estate Employers cater to the needs of his community. His word is law! At his command, Indian Tamil labour in Sri Lanka resorts to their latest tactic, the powerful 'Go Slow

'Movement'! They do not strike like earlier and turn up, but work very slowly so have to be paid minimum wages! The exasperated management can do nothing and is forced to negotiate, to prevent massive losses!

The President, Sri Lanka Estate Employer's Federation Mr.R.L.Harvey, British Manager, Demodera Group, organizes the publication of a first time ever Tamil newspaper on any estate, for the welfare of the employees. The Tamil Assistant Manager Rajah Brodie is the editor of The Demodera Digest in name, but ¹ studiedLatin instead of Tamil, so his wife Lalitha is in full charge! This is her first taste of service and she goes for it heart and soul! She edits and re-writes enthusiastic contributions from the workers and members of staff, introduces a women's page, educational material on health, prevention of disease etc. After a few months, she translates into Tamil literature from her fmehel Mrs. Sundarasen at the Badulla hospital about the latest Oral Contraceptives, just introduced into Sri Lanka. Even members of staff are surprised and advice her that those pills are not meant

to be swallowed! The Demodera Manjari gets a lot
of praise and rave reviews in the Tamil Media!

Thondaman, alarmed that the Management is trying to
win over the allegiance of the labour force, forbids
them from purchasing the paper, selling for 10 cents!
They blindly obey him! What a pity!
After ten monthly issues, The Management saves face
by stopping the publication of the paper, when Mr and
Mrs Rajah Brodie are granted four months furlough
leave abroad, in February 1964!

37. RADIO ASIA CANADA (ITR)
International Tamil Radio
20.12.1997

Wow! Konesh, Padmini, Pradeep & Radhika have
done it again! What another marvellous achievement
this is in the annals of AMCC/Radio Asia Canada,
after all the name and fame of being the very first to
start Tamil radio broadcasts from scratch, for an hour
in Canada, from a basement!

Our majestic eagle has set new horizons
to soar forward in service with pride and joy!

Of-course once again, as the very first Tamil Media
to outreach internationally for the full twenty-four
hours into the homes, workplaces and vehicles
of every single individual South Asian Tamil
in every nook and corner of the whole wide world!

Radio Asia does not target Mars, Moon or Jupiter
but only to explore the universe of the human mind!
Our aim is to win over every single brother and sister
to nurture our language, music, heritage and culture
endeavour to raise self-esteem, empathy and awareness
with education, knowledge, strength and skill
and guide everyone to reach their full potential
toward acceptance, peace, harmony and happiness.

We envision introducing several brand new surprise
facets to enhance our Radio Programs and God willing
may step into the world of TV too in the near future!

38. OSTEOPOROSIS

It is December 1996, and I feel fine.
However, my belated tests reveal that
I have severe bone disease, osteoporosis!

After my 1981 hysterectomy, scoliosis
has silently crept up to slowly curve my spine.
I hunch and have become five inches shorter
and have lost forty-six percent of my bone density!

How is it that not one around me saw this change?
I know that I am not this mortal body alone
and am the eternal spirit living in this transient abode.
However I yet feel so vibrant and young at heart
and wish to accomplish so much more in life. . .

This jolts me to realise that my body is aging fast
and my time on earth is really running out.
I am not a complainer and have always tried
to accept my lot as life unfolds around me.
I will accept this too and am grateful that I yet feel
alright and can travel by bus to broadcast my weekly
two hour Personal Growth program over Radio Asia
to disseminate education and information on varied
subjects and about prevention of osteoporosis too ...

However now at last, there is a lot of hope
My December 1997 tests reveal
an increase of 5% in bone density!
Thanks to God and The Better Bones Better Health

Osteoporosis Pilot Program, and the dedication
of our teachers at Humber River Regional Hospital
where I am a volunteer from 1992 till now.

39. DIVORCE

Despite all frantic efforts
divorce somehow manages
to creep in regardless
into our beloved families
and I find it so difficult
to meekly accept this
unwelcome change . . .

Even at this threshold
of the millennium,
has our eastern culture
so over-conditioned me
to make me believe
that the binding vows
of fidelity and chastity
in marriage are sacred?

I do firmly believe
that marriage is a journey

of two individuals,
like two rugged stones
placed together in a can,
drawn along on the road
and shaken about hard
with the specific purpose
to smooth the rough
edges of each other.

Discarding partners
will definitely bring forth
different rough surfaces
with the pressing need
to be smoothed
all over once again!

40. HOLIDAY 1998

The two-month holiday, all on my own
with ten days at Puttaparthi, India!
All the frills of life fall
and only the bare essentials
remain in vogue here!
I do exactly what I choose!
For just ten rupees per day

I sleep on a thin mattress on the floor
among the women in the Foreigner's shed
and listen to the multicultural symphony
of the various foreign tongues.
Busy anthills bother some
while an insect hopping in the dark
scares another, who shouts
"An animal is jumping here!".!

But all are happy, at peace
with themselves and with everyone else.
Friendliness abounds around me. . .
Everyone keeps busy!
No one tries to impress the other!
We remain just our very own selves
simple spiritual seekers
from around the globe
clamouring for progress
on the pilgrim's way . . .

Bhagavan Sathya Sai Baba appears
four times a day and there is
pin-drop silence among
more than 25 000 devotees!
The area reverberates with adoration!

His words are vibrations of Love, Truth
Peace, Non-violence and Right Conduct
which effectively proclaim
His message to humanity!
I greedily lap up as much as I can
and recharge my spiritual batteries.
The soul-stirring singer starts
leading the morning bhajans
and we join singing along in chorus.
Why do I feel so much at home here?
This pulsing, astounding sanctity
touches, pervades and rejuvenates
my body, mind, emotions and soul
and satiated, I leave for Sri Lanka.

Colombo appears smaller and poorer.
No new buildings, nor any sign of progress!
The war is sapping up all effort and energy!
Yet, it is so good to tread this soil once again.
I do feel so sad that there is absolutely
no transport to Jaffna, my beloved hometown.
But the sight, love and inter-action
of family and friends in the capital
amply compensates, while as usual
whirlwind time regardless hurries past.

I decide to discard the privacy
of the speeding three wheelers
that manage to zigzag so cutely
through the choc-a-bloc traffic!
I travel along with the crowds
the Tamil 'pottu' flaunting my forehead
and talk with many a passenger
in the bulging buses and vans.
I am well rewarded as people open up
and are as friendly as ever . . .

I well remember the middle-aged, sarong clad
stranger in the bus beside his wife in Kandyan saree
their body language clearly proclaiming their
intimacy, offering me peanuts. We start talking in
Sinhalese and alight at the same bus stop.
"We are having lunch at this 'kade'!
Will you join us please?"
Invites this friendly mechanic.

And again in the speeding mini-van
an old person in white national garb
who gives me his seat, waits,
and escorts me inside his work-place
the palatial Lake House
the core of the National Media.

I well know that fear is the companion
always living with the Tamils in Colombo!
But it's indeed lovely to realize that the basic
goodness of people somehow still manages
to remain unchanged and is very much the same
in spite of all the suffering, the scars of war and
the shocking crime spiralling daily!
How is it, that life appears so serene on the
surface, while the bitter conflict continues?
Have they got so used to the war?
Or is it my grey hair and fluency
in Sinhalese that elicits such kindness?

Another day in December
tropical torrents, try to wash
the face of Colombo
as I wend my way home
under the battered umbrella
after the crowded bus ride.
Slippers greet me, afloat on the lawn
and as usual, I begin to compare
"It never pours, does it
like this in Ontario?"

"Hey! What a surprise!
My handbag is neatly cut!

Theivika's X'mas present
the thousand-rupee note
within her card is missing!"
I wonder about the need
that prompted this pickpocket!
And the expertise with which
only the note vanished!
However, I just can't imagine
which person out of the well-dressed
crowd standing so close around me
was the clever culprit?

41. CHASTITY

Eastern epics extol
the virtues of women
in hard to believe tales . . .
Ancient Nalayini carried
her crippled husband
in a basket on her head
to the prostitute,
to fulfil his wish!

Kannaki, furious
that the king

unjustly beheaded
her errant husband, Kovalan
burnt the city of Madurai!
Her chastity and fidelity
bestowed on her the power
to command the elements
in retaliation . . .

Savithri's chastity gave her
the power, to follow
and gain back the life
of her dead husband Sathyavan
from the Lord of death, Yama!

But, wait a minute!
What about chastity
for the men too?

42. FEELINGS

I am well aware
that the human spirit eternal
will never age or perish
and I do know that

the mind and the body
will falter with age.
However surprise does
taunt me, when I find
that now my elderly emotions
seem to play up too!

Why is it that my feelings
now fail to react strongly
when confronted with
the widespread violence
in the world, erupting
like volcanoes everywhere?
Have I got so used
to violence, that it no longer
surprises me, as it used to earlier?

Mass-media screams
"Tamil Mother and dead children
discovered in car trunk"
"Thirteen young Tamil,
suicide black tigers
blow themselves up
along with thirteen planes
immobilizing Katunayake,
the main airport in Sri Lanka"!

I feel really sad
that my Tamil community
yet shuns psychotherapy.
Unfortunately, everyone
around her failed to recognize
the symptoms, to seek remedy
for the pain and suffering
of that bereaved mother!
What a crushing shame
that the Norwegian peace efforts
of Eric Solheim collapsed.
The terror of war and destruction
stalks my people once again.
Oh God! Please guide me!
What and what I can do
to prevent this escalating violence
that has wiped out
a whole young generation
in my beloved motherland?

I can only cry out
for help once again,
to the leaders of the world!
Oh come! You the United Nations
and the Great Powers of the World!

Why not at least now, intervene
in this prolonging conflict
and negotiate with both opponents
for an acceptable solution
so that a Just Peace would blossom
to end all this terror and bloodshed
in Sri Lanka as well as in
all the other war plagued lands?

26.7.2001

43. UNEXPECTED

It's the last day of January 2001.
The severe snow storm suddenly strikes,
breaking the unusual spring-like weather.
Despite all the storm warnings
my addiction to the Broadcast urges me,
and I manage to travel by TTC as usual
planning to hire a taxi from Finch Ave.
to avoid the short walk down Tapscott
and risk breaking some more of my bones.

However, what a lovely surprise!
Petite teen-aged co-traveller, pretty Melissa

140

from Guyana, volunteers far out of her way!
I request her help only to cross the road,
but she takes my hand and escorts me
through the slippery snow for twenty minutes
to ITBC MEDIANET in time for my weekly
two hour Live Radio and TV Talk Shows!

It is such a pity that we Tamils live so secluded
and do not mix a lot with other communities.
Shouldn't we try to change our habits little by little?
What better proof than this episode, that goodness
does prevail in-spite of all relevant negativity,
entwining different strands of so many communities
into the magnificent tapestry of global humanity!

44. LOVE

Love is the pulsing elixir of life
for without love, life is so barren.
We are born as embodiments of love
but we forget that and cloak ourselves

with cruel negativity, which begets
all the problems that plague us today.

When awareness finally dawns
and we realize our mistake
we are too old and it is too late
as we are near the doors of death!

45. LOVE AND BEAUTY

A thing of beauty is indeed a joy forever,
but have you noticed that beautiful women
have always had turbulent lives?

Their beauty is more of an enemy than a friend!
Let us leave the famous ancient beauties
like Helen of Troy, Sita, Ahaliya and the rest aside.
Even in this 21st century, why does a beautiful wife
without fail, evoke paranoid jealousy in her husband?

46. LIFE 2002

I feel sad that Dorothy Hahn is gone.
She was a lovely person, and it is a pity that
we, OWN writers will never again hear
that gentle voice reading delightful and touching
stories about her life in Toronto and Montreal.

Two of my Jaffna Chundikuli classmates too
recently stepped beyond into the unknown.
I feel so guilty that I did not call Thiru Sivaps
in Boston more often, though I should have,
when she boldly faced her challenges of health.
In the forties, from Grade Three to Ten,
we three musketeers from Chundikuli,
tomboyish Thiru, pretty Valli and me,
daily walked, chatting gay and carefree,
up and down four times in the blazing sun,
tempting young Secretariat officers
to wait and watch us from upstairs windows,
a belated surprise revealed to me in 1989
by a colleague at Counseling Center Shanthiyaham!

I wonder how much more time I have on earth.
My body is deteriorating rapidly and I do hope

that I will not become a burden to anyone
and can depart with ease when my time arrives.
I pause in retrospect and reflect
on the many different paths and phases
I have crossed during my life so far,
before arriving here in Canada in 1992.

I am happy and quite content
to be here, where I am now today.
I have just two years more
to reach the biblical three score and ten
and have completed fifty years of marriage!
Rajah and I are as different as the two poles
and though we tread completely different paths
still somehow manage to pull along together.
Our marriage is an excellent example that
divorce is not the best solution for
family troubles!
Unconditional love, empathetic
understanding
and forgiveness will elicit
similar feelings
which will iron out most of the
problems.

47. VISION

Thank you dear God, for restoring my vision fully
through the healing hands of the best in the world,
gentle genius Dr.Steve Arshinoff at Humber River
Regional Hospital, on November 14th 2002.
Starting the double cataract surgery, the doctor
quips,"Lecturing in Mysore, India recently I was
at Lalitha Mahal, fabulous palace of the former
Maharajah". Wide-awake under local anaesthesia,
I butt in, "You went so close, yet didn't visit
Sri Sathya Sai Baba? Next time you must definitely
volunteer your expertise in Puttarparthi
and Bangalore, at Baba's Super Specialty Hospitals".
"Stop talking! Your eye is moving", cautions the
doctor and I close my big mouth shut, till the end
of the forty-minute surgery. At the post-operative
eye test the next morning, vision in my right eye
is ok but my left draws a complete blank!
The doctor says that my cornea is inflamed
but should be alright. I sadly wonder whether
my moving lips had harmed the surgery. . .

I know that I am a spiritual being in this physical
experience of life. I have surrendered myself into
God's hands for sometime now, accepting and

coping with everything that comes my way,
battling even some unexpected challenges that
trouble me, yet regardless somehow manage
to carry on. I start to muse, "If it is my destiny
to be one-eyed for the rest of my life, I will have
to accept this too", I console myself.
"Why can't I, if so many others can set examples,
especially visually handicapped friends in Toronto,
Srikamalan, Praba, Jothy and Thurai who are doing
well, so joyfully working and caring for their families?

Dr.Archinoff agrees to come on my TV program
next year and gives a CD-Disc illustrating how
unique his technique is, compared to cataract
surgery half a century ago, when patients
were hospitalized with motionless head
sandwiched betwixt sandbags for a week!
No restrictions at all now. One can even shower
or do anything except lift heavy weights.
 However for a record, I am glad I did not
view his CD-Disc earlier, for if I had, I may not
have ventured to participate in that three-day
ONPEA-Ontario Network For The Prevention
of Elder Abuse in downtown, Toronto by bus,
and subway, adorned in dark glasses,
just four days after twin cataract surgery!

146

48. CANADA DAY
1.7.2002

Happy Birthday! Happy 135th Birthday, O Canada!
We, members of The Senior Tamil Center, Ontario,
gather to greet you today with great love and joy.
Our voices rise together to praise you with a
brimming heart as our gratitude gushes forth
like the cascading Niagara, for what you have
already done and yet continue to do for us.
When we had to flee our war-ravaged motherland,
you magnanimously opened your doors wide to
welcome, grant refuge and a brand new life for us all,
numbering well over three hundred thousand now.

Our habitually hard working hands and sharp minds
keep busy as ever here too, as we slowly blend in to
enrich the vast, vibrant mosaic of your multicultural
mainstream. We are proud of all our achievements
in your bosom so far and we assure you, we'll continue
to endeavour with all our might to bedeck and adorn
you with more and more dazzling jewels of our skilled
enterprise and expertise in every possible field.

The dove of Peace hovers ever so slowly over
our homeland now and we await its descent with

abated breath and expectant hearts. Air-flights are
daily packed now as our people flock to Tamil
Eelam to visit precious relatives, well loved
homes, and habitual haunts . . .

Oh! How I long to step on the soil of my beloved
Tamil Eelam, the land of my birth, joyful
childhood and youth, once again!
Oh! To breathe the air of freedom, to taste
the food, the fish and the fruit, the mouth watering
kool, karuvadu, karuppani rice, kurakkan pittu,
the delectable 'illuppai-poo urundai, ural-pounded
manioc and sambol', the special mutton and
delicious seafood from the Columbuthurai lagoon . . .
I visualize with nostalgia, the pervading piety
in our sea-side St.Anthony's church!
How lovely it'll be to worship Nallur Kanthan
at His annual chariot festival, as bakthas devotion,
kavadis and bhajans sanctify the surroundings!
Our patient wait outside, awaiting the appearance of
the adorned deities, borne aloft on the bare
shirtless shoulders of eager young men,
while flaming camphor and broken
coconuts signify vanishing egos.
Our joy in joining to pull the bedecked chariot

around the temple, the carnival atmosphere,
the rows of hundreds of small make-shift shops,
the jostling crowds, the shopping spree and the busy
bargaining battle all of us indulge in, during the
latter part of the twenty-five day festivals.
Our trek back home chatting, crunching fresh
roasted hot corn, kadalai and peanuts!

It is lovely to be back from Eelam in time for this
Canada Day celebration today!
It is indeed great that Canada has gifted us
so much, to raise our standard of living.
What can we give in return to show our gratitude
to our gracious benefactor?
We can sure contribute a lot so that we leave
not only Canada, but the world too a better place!

Why not first lobby for nominated Tamil MP's,
to voice our concerns, as we are scattered
and cannot elect our own Tamil representatives
to the Canadian parliament?
It's a pity that abuse and violence stealthily
stalk almost every community and the mass-media
daily abounds with shocking reports about the worst
of humanity! Seniors, so respected back at home,

are crushed by the reversal of status here,
the taunts of children and even grandchildren
amidst the generation gap, relationship conflicts,
climatic and lifestyle changes, the denial of
qualifications, expertise and experience, the
language barrier, transportation and mobility,
living space, privacy, isolation/loneliness,
awareness/access to adequate home-care
and to available Legal Aid, plus hiding the
trauma of female menopause and male andropause,
without accepting the transience of this physical
sheath, which is the cause of all problems
which hinder graceful aging and spirituality.
What can and what should every one of us do
to stem this downward trend?

We have just this one chance to live!
Let us utilize all our faculties to the utmost,
Practice the Human Values of Love, Truth,
Right-conduct, Peace and Non-violence
and daily nurture our personal growth, to realize
our full potential as human beings.
O come! Let everyone of us make resolve today
to strengthen in balanced manner, not only
our body and mind, but the pining spirit too,

so that our self-esteem will soar and the need
for violence to exert power and control
to bolster our ego disappears for good.
We must realize that we are actually
spiritual beings in a physical experience!
Neither do we bring or take back anything
with us, so we must not lead too materialistic lives.
The best recipe for prevention and eradication
of all negativity in the world today is boosting
Individual Personal Growth, which will ensure
Happy Families, Healthy Communities
Harmonious Nations, Universal Spirituality
culminating in a Vibrant Humanity.

49. EXPLORATION OF SPACE
1.2.2003

Farewell, beloved astronaut martyrs
of the ill-fated Columbia!
You, the seven selfless sovereigns
of supreme sacrifice for science!
You the multicultural maestros,
who risked your all for humanity!
What a shame your space shuttle
orbit venture of sixteen days,

should vanish in vain like vapour,
just sixteen minutes before touch down!

That invasive culprit Fear, somehow
often manages to confront,
confine and crowd us like zombies
into dark, desolate corners.
Pray, how did you succeed
in winning over your instincts
and emotions and conquer
every selfish whim, to rise
as eternal heroes in history?

Exploration and expansion are no doubt
essentials for growth of any kind.
We, chest thumbing addicts,
will of course continue the conquest
of space at any cost and will never stop.
We did conquer the moon and mars quite
sometime ago, but what did we gain?
We just had a glimpse of the earth
from space, that was all, no other benefits!
Don't you think that we must change
our focus a little at least, to unveil the glory
of our eternal spirit, analyse and control

the bottomless depths of our unruly mind,
unveil the true aim of life and stem
the downward spiral of humanity
before proceeding any further in space?
Will it not be more productive
if our Super Powers make resolve
to first explore the vast universe of the
human mind and the languishing spirit?

50.   PETS & OTHER ISSUES
2005

The bored look of the lone fighter fish
languishing in its small glass globe, reminds me
of my first unsuccessful attempt in 1956,
at rearing fish in a bottle at Rajah Estate!
I then didn't know that fish need greens to live!
My kids and I sadly watched the frantic efforts
of the panicking fish to breathe, mistaking
that they sought to escape from the bottle!

Of-course I too have gone through the mill!
Like everyone else I did have my retinue
of pets - parrots, love birds, cats, dogs, poultry,

goats and even cows as we roamed the large
tea estates. I even tried my hand at Bonsai,
semi-starving plants in shallow pots with
impoverished soil till cousin Dharma said,
"You turned vegetarian as you don't wish to
hurt life, but how come you abuse vegetation
and dwarf plants for pleasure and money?"

Yes! Beginning meditation in 1983 did hone my
intellect and I who loved non-veg, changed radically.
I now realize that intruding into other lives is unfair.
Having pets only fulfills our own pressing selfish need
to have power and control over our relationships!
It is now an accepted and flourishing form of abuse
and the pet industry has conquered hearts globally.
Toronto alone boasts of thirty-nine pet shops!
A variety of pets including snakes and chameleons,
do provide their owners not only the means to express
love, but also grant the opportunity to exercise their
power and control at their every whim and fancy?

It is argued that without castration and birth control
pets will breed prolifically and create utter chaos!
But I feel that this is a forerunner for so many weird matters.
Mass cloning of crops was followed by the creation of

Dolly the sheep plus God only knows what and what else!
Quest for the cure of disease makes organ donation
and stem cell research seem alright in our selfish minds!
We do find it tough, don't we, to accept the truth that
the spirit is eternal and aging and death of the body have
to be accepted as unavoidable natural processes of life?

The name Terry somehow seems to attract attention!
Young Terry Fox created history with his one-legged
world marathon for cancer research.25 years ago!
Terri Schavio created history in 2005, winning her
husband's long-drawn conflict with her parents for her to die
with dignity without life support in her vegetative state!
When and where are we going to stop trying to play God
mimicking creation? The ever-widening vicious
cycle spirals on regardless. I wonder
when humanity will awaken to the truth to
become more aware of the cruelty perpetrated when
we interfere in other lives and try our best to negate
the process of nature!

51. TSUNAMI SPEAKING!
26.12.2004

"Hi Humanity! I am the Tsunami!
Will you please listen to me!
I am sorry, truly so very sorry
for what happened
within those few minutes!
Please do forgive me!
I know how you are cursing me
saying, "Sumatra born Tsunami!
Tell me, do tell me at once!
Why did you stealthily surface
so suddenly, without any warning
to claim so many lives?
So much of destruction
and loss amongst eleven nations!
We cannot comprehend
how the very elements
that grant and support life
can so cruelly rise in unison
to orchestrate all this annihilation!"

Please stop it! I have had enough
of your tirades. My outburst was

really an out-pouring of my anger!
Nature's anger at the foibles
of humanity! Nature chooses harsh
methods to teach lessons! Earth quakes,
volcanoes, floods, tornados, typhoons!
You know how earlier tsunamis
have swallowed up whole cities.
I was literally forced to surface
after the earth quake in Sumatra.
I couldn't help it! Do you think that I
creating this enjoy colossal calamity?
I tell you again, I just couldn't help it!

I was happy when humanity did take heed
and joined together in global harmony,
with outpourings of empathy support and relief.
But alas, look what is happening now?
Things are back to square zero once again
I am not sure when and how humanity
is going to learn to mend at least some
of the mistakes and attempt
to live in peace and harmony with nature!

IV. FAMILY

52. MY STORY

The Human spirit eternal proceeds on its pilgrim's
way, leaving guiding footprints, on the sands of
time! How very true it is in life, that what we do
know is only a tiny fistful, while the unknown
is limitless! I realise this more and more every day
in my life, of the Here and the Now.

I celebrate life, hold my head high and am truly
glad and grateful to be what I am today!
I have accepted and coped with the ups and downs
of my allotted life and am aware of my limitations.
Like driftwood, I first floated with my parents
and three sisters Chandra, Ranji and Leela
then joined my husband. I wonder from
where they came and how they chose me,
but our five children joined us, and I realise
how lucky I am to be thus blest, with this
inimitable gift of five children, with such fine
personalities! I have no favourites and feel
the same love and devotion for every one of them,
though I am sure they are bound to disagree!

Each child is so different from the other, like
the five fingers of my hand! My only daughter,
clever and musical Nirmala, so graceful and pretty
was followed fifteen months later by fair and tall
eldest son Niranjan, good-hearted though quick to
temper. Quiet and loving introvert Ravi, resembling
Rajah came after two years, born in the astrological
time of Venus, when I too had the same period,
and the combination may have elevated our life!
We built our house in Jaffna and moved to the
Whittal Boustead Company job on Demodera Group,
where naughty and cheerful Ajantha, so different
to the others appeared after four years. Two years
later the last of the lot, sloe-eyed Aravindha, full
of incessant chatter and laughter completed my family.

Life on Demodera was good with lots of benefits,
but had a very big setback! We had to send the
children away to boarding schools from Grade One!
All of them yet resent this and blame me, but there
was no other available choice then, if we wanted
good education for our kids! Though young
and immature I did the very best I could for them,
and I am really happy and proud that all my children

have blossomed out to be such excellent adults.
With time they left the fold, started their own lives
with partners and children and I feel so happy
when I take turns and rotate between their homes!
Eleven talented grandchildren are now mine to love
and adore without responsibility, and I may be lucky
to meet my great-grandchildren too before my exit!

Yes! It is now time to reflect that in the end, I have
to float alone, like every single life into the unknown!
Nothing do we bring or take with us, but our karma!
Of course, I have genuinely blundered so many times
and have often offended even those very dear to me!
I have now matured to accept my mistakes and apologise!
I always forgive and forget, harbour no grudges, hatred
or regrets in life as I have always tried to accomplish
the very best that I can in all what I touch around me.
I have no guilt, am at peace with my own self as I feel
the spark within and the guiding hand of that Great
Omnipotent Power That is God on my shoulder.
I may wander and stumble but have absolute faith,
that He will never let me fall! He knows me in and out,
as I accept His will and am in tune with Him! I feel His
strength perennial, filling me with grace and my vessel
overflows.

53. IN MEMORIAM
V.A.Nadarajah 1907 – 1971

May 1971
What shall I write of thee, my dear Appah?
What shall I write about thee?
Shall I say how very much I miss thee
Now that thou art no more?
A mild man of high morals and integrity
gone suddenly without final farewells
into the unknown, a month ago
quietly and gently as thou lived!

You always worked far away in Colombo
and I never did have enough of thy company . . .
I picked up a lot of thy habits,
thy patience and thy forbearance
and am a bookworm too like thee!
Oh! How I wish I could have had thee
thy wisdom, knowledge and guidance
for just a few years more!

But solace descends when I realize
that Thee, the eternal, omnipresent spirit
art at constant watch, and will definitely

guide every single one of us,
Ammah, Chandra, Ranji, Leela
me and my family in all our efforts
till it is time for us to join thee.

54. AMMAH – 1998

I visualise you every morning, ammah dear
though you are in Colombo, so far away.
Oh! My carefree childhood in Ariyalai
in grandma's cosy thatched three-piece house!
I remember your love and care and specially,
you in dressed up elegance happily walking
to the temple festivals with Appah,
young and graceful in your silk saree. . .

Appah was your cousin, love and life, wasn't he?
You wrote letters to him every single day
and correspondence kept your romance alive!
He always worked far away, all over the isle
as a roving Govt. Superintendent of Audits
and came home for only fleeting weekends . . .
How Chandra and I used to race down our lane
to the railway tracks, when we heard

the morning coal mail train puff and coo!
I can still see Appah's broad smile and wave
and yet taste the orange candy he threw for us . . .

I remember your tear-drenched face with your
long hair loose and uncombed as you worried for
Appah's life, when Japan bombed Colombo in 1941
I also well remember your annoyance when I
brought home an abandoned pup and when I always
curled up and read away, never helping you with
the housework. I remember the tiny hut that Appah
made for us and the manioc flour pittu, rice and curry
that we cooked on real fire, in tiny earthen pots and pans!
Absence does make the heart grow fonder indeed ...

Appah built palatial upstairs No.86 Kandy Rd. in
1943 and we shifted near the Kachcheri and our
College in 1946. How very proud of your new home
You were Ammah! You spent such a lot of time
cleaning and sweeping the compound and the curries
would be often bubbling on the fire when we came
for lunch. You were an excellent cook. Your delectable
oil cakes make my mouth water when I think of
them. My four sons were really lucky to enjoy your
love and care in their senior years at St.Johns'
College during their short sojourn in Jaffna.

164

Life never materialises making dreams come true!
Appah retired, but alas, he never lived long
enough to enjoy your company and his beloved
collection of books. After Appah, you changed so
much Ammah! You became just a recluse, cook
and housekeeper. You didn't want to get out
anywhere, foolishly we too agreed and you spent all
your time only within your house and compound . . .

Years have simply whizzed past! Your body is frail
and feeble now at 84, but your mind is yet so sharp
and you still write such lovely letters Ammah!
It's great that you have come out unscathed
after all the trials and trauma from the war zone!
No doubt, you must be missing your beloved house
full of memories and treasured belongings!
You must be longing to get back
to dear old Jaffna!
I eagerly look forward to my
holiday with you
darling Ammah, we will sit
and talk, talk and talk ...

55. AMMAMMAH
1893 – 1983

I never did tell you, what a great influence you
have been in my life, did I Ammammah? With little
education, you were so wise and full of knowledge.
You were adorned with beauty, health, high morals,
helpful ways and an extrovert personality.
Everyone in the Ariyalai held you in high esteem,
looked up to you and luckily I did pick up a lot
from you to follow in your footsteps.

Born as the only girl with three brothers in Govt.
service, you married early. You were a young
widow with seven small children when you lost
your beloved Nagalingam suddenly. I remember
you sharing with teen-aged me, how you tended
him with love and care as he lay mortally ill with
diarrhoea. He was a farmer and cigar trader but he
was your love. I well remember the excellent feasts
you prepared for his almsgivings after the rituals by
the priest. You had paddy fields, cows, goats and
poultry and were always busy as a bee with one
thing and another. Trials and tribulations
strengthened you and you deftly handled your
challenges. Of-course your brothers and in-laws

must have helped you and when Appah married
Ammah he took the burden off your shoulders.

I remember you all dressed up fair, petite and
pretty, with your large ruby earrings, gold attiyal
throatlet, in one of your two silk sarees that I
remember – the white silk with the pink and blue
border and the yellow kurunadu. I remember
Chandra and me taking turns to massage your
aching legs as you reclined with your cigar on the
deerskin on the cow dung treated 'thinnai'/verandah
of your three piece, thatched mud cottage. You told
me great stories about a famine when people had to
boil straw and drink, as there was no rice and to learn
to be always frugal! Also how the cobra spits out
its precious emerald to hunt by the light, while
waiting men on trees, drop cow dung on the
gem to grab it!

You were a leader in social work too. You helped
all the Ariyalai contestants like Casipillai,
Ponnambalam and A.M.Brodie in municipal
elections, coaxing, herding and accompanying
voters in Austin hiring cars. Your children loved,
respected and obeyed you implicitly. I can picture

you smearing protesting Kuttimama Thurairajah's tonsils with 'pirandai thandu' (a wild cactus like creeper) and salt which made his inflamed tonsils to simply melt away without surgery! You also regularly poured doses of castor oil down all our reluctant throats! When I joined teacher uncle Gunaratnam to Sri Parvathy Vithiyasalai, you would bring lunch and feed me through the small gate.

You were a splendid cook and made for us every old-fashioned eatable unknown to most modern folks. You faithfully made odial and oothuma kool, odial and kurakkan pittu, karuppani rice, lime pickle, achcharu, and vadaham plus the seasonal 'panaatu' by spreading and drying layers of palmyrah fruit juice on a mat. You also made us spread mats under the towering illuppai (olive like) trees in bloom and collect the pearly, honey sweet flowers in the mornings. You pounded these dried flowers in the ural (mortar & pestle) with chillies and I remember those delectable sweet/spicy balls and sesame seed balls with nostalgia. Uncle Gunam was keen vegetable gardener and you often made tasty balls of chilli-coconut-sambol and pounded boiled manioc for a hearty meal.

You gave your house to Mahes ammah and
Sithappah Nadarajah as dowry and shifted with
Sothy ammah and uncle Sivaguru when we moved
to our upstairs house at 86 (now 147) Kandy Road.
You often walked down the railway tracks to our
house to help ammah in the cooking. I am happy
that you travelled out of Jaffna at least a couple of
times on holiday and stayed with me on Panilkande
and Rajah estates, Deniyaya. You helped ammah to
look after Chandra when she had Theivika and me
during my five confinements. You would massage
the noses and bodies of our babies with special
medicated kiranthi oil, let them kick on a mat
in the morning sun and later bathe them.

You attended the weddings of two of your great
grand children Nirmala and Ravi and were there to
greet great great grandchildren, Nisha, Ramana,
Pavithra and Ranga! You lived up to a ripe old age
of 90 years and grandson Kanthi (Umakanthan
Sivaguru) tended you with love and care in your
twilight years.
My darling Ammammah! I will forever
Remember you with fondest love and gratitude.

169

56. THE MAN IN MY LIFE
RAJAH BRODIE

Happy Birthday! Happy Birthday!
Wish you a very Happy Birthday
and many Happy Returns of 18.8.2001!
Fifty Years! Fifty Years!
It is fifty years since I met you!
You'll remember how you intercepted
and totally changed my life in 1951.
Ever since then, I am sure you will agree
that I have always done my very best
in thought, word and deed for you,
our children, their partners and grandchildren

My life with you is an open book
and when I turn its pages, I find
that though I was a teen-aged bride
I changed, to run along keeping pace
with you to the best of my ability,
though we are so different to each other.
We have faced several challenges together
but always managed to cope pretty well!

We were forced to board our children, to give
them education in prestigious schools, otherwise

we had it good with all material comforts on estates.
We had to face our share of crises in life
but with divine grace, always overcame difficulties
which made me turn more toward spirituality.

You did look after me with concern and care
first after my hysterectemy in Kamdy in 1981,
and later when I rose from the clutches of death
in Colombo, after the mini-bus knocked me down,
with three unconsious days in hospital, fractures
of an arm, seven ribs and a collapsed lung,
confined to bed almost immobile for a month
before travelling by ambulance, home to Jaffna.

We made Canada our second home in 1992.
You took pride in working as a security guard.
After retirement you, who as a tea planter
never had time to look after your own children
did enjoy caring for our Canadian grandchildren!
You were given a big surprise 75 th. birthday party
and I had a real surprise with my 70 th in 2004!
You have lived as you wished all along,
with yearly holidays in Sri Lanka.
Both of us are now on our last lap in the race of life.
Though I still feel young at heart, I am well aware

that my time on earth is really running out.

I am now passionate about writing and broadcasting and I am trying to do what I feel I really ought to do! Thanks a lot for giving me the freedom to do all what I want to accomplish before my final exit!.

57.   RELATIONSHIPS

I've been requested to write on relationships for Mothers Day, by The Toronto Asian Heritage Festival, May 1997.

What is life, but a continuing interaction of individuals between alternating periods of pleasure and pain? Like the interwoven tapestry of the ever-changing seasons, are our lives entwined intricately into our relationships. Live alone, we seldom or never do. We do need the other, to live as a pair and team together with kith and kin, to care and share amongst family, friend and foe, relative and partner, acquaintance and colleague, master and neighbour. But most important of all, with the innermost core of our very own selves, that spark of the divine our conscience, the omnipresent God within, that eternal witness, to our every thought, word and deed.

Every one of us strives toward happy relationships,
that vitally essential, but quicksilver ingredient,
which precedes contentment, success, peace and joy.

However try as we may, harmony always eludes us!
Why do we forever bump into such unexpected trouble?
Somehow misunderstanding and mishaps crop up
and mushroom into angry, revenge seeking conflicts,
that continue to mar our lives with many a scar!
Does destiny thus confront, and seek to guide us,
only to ensure that we nurture the basic human values,
and genuinely learn to live with them from childhood?
Unconditional Love, Truth, Peace and Non-violence,
that led us to tread the track of Right Conduct,
focus on the balanced growth of the spirit too,
instead of pampering only the demands of the body,
and the insatiable lure of the me and the mine.
Place a ceiling on the desires of the fickle mind
and thus, raise the self esteem of every single individual,
so that first we can love and accept our very own selves,
dip inside, share our unconditional love and acceptance
in ample measure with every person around us.

This personal growth of the self-esteem of every
individual, will negate the need for abuse to gain

control and power to feel good. This will lead us
toward the true goals of human life, Self- actualisation
and joyful Self-realization which will ensure
happy families, healthy communities
progressive nations and a harmonious humanity.

58. MOTHERS AND DAUGHTERS

Motherhood is sacred beyond
measure,
God's greatest gift to us women,
as we become almost one with
the creator,
when we actively participate in
this miracle,
gladly giving of our body, mind,
and the spirit

so caringly and unselfishly
for nine long months
making our very own
brand new baby . . .

Out of the blue in nineteen
fifty-two

came arranged marriage and love to me
followed immediately by teenaged motherhood!
I yet remember my marvel and joy
when I first beheld my firstborn, my only daughter.
I gazed and gazed at her tiny fair face
her perfect proportion, thick jet-black hair
and fully-grown finger and toenails
and at once forgot all the pain of childbirth . . .

I was lucky to have my maternal instincts enriched
and enhanced by my caring grandmother and
mother. Sweet little Nirmala blossomed forth
and was the adorable darling of the family,
till I had my four sons in quick succession.
Niranjan, Ravindran, Ajantha and Aravintha!
Five big, bonny babies within nine years!
A strange situation this present era of mothers,
with well established parenthood patterns,
will find it difficult to imagine even in their dreams!

Of course I never appreciated it at that time and longed
for a good nights' sleep, the rest and the leisure . . .
However I now realise what a precious time
of giving it was, as definitely those have
been the best years of my life.

At five, little Nirmala had to become a boarder
far away at prestigious St.Bridgets' Convent,
Colombo. However the boys could come home
for weekends as they were at St.Thomas' Prep.
Bandarawela nearer home, the 3200 acre largest
Sri Lankan Tea Estate Demodera Group.
My little girl must have felt very resentful and sad
that we favoured her four brothers, while she
had to be away from home for such long periods.
She was too small to understand my plight,
as then I never travelled alone and as manager
in charge, Rajah had the perennial difficulty of leave!
However my daughter did make me proud!
She made her mark, shone in all her endeavours
and became a polished product of the Convent.

On swift wings flew time, fulfilling destiny . . .
Nirmala made a most beautiful bride, and in turn
was blessed with the cutest bundle of joy
beloved eldest grandchild mine, my darliing Nisha.
I felt that Nisha was my very own, my second
daughter. She too clung to me as I lavished all
my attention and care, till pretty granddaughters
Pavithra, and Kanjana appeared on the scene.
Grandchildren are great gifts, giving such sheer

pleasure, ours to love, cuddle, enjoy, spoil and adore
without the rigours and responsibilities of parenthood.

Five generations of mothers and daughters!
My grandma, ma, daughter and granddaughter
Sinnammah, Nallammah, Lalitha, Nirmala and
Nsha! With elation we posed for that lovely
family portrait! A rare treasure of our family
lineage and heritage that we cherished and
displayed with great pride. But alas! That
memento is now lost to us for ever, along with
almost every single thing that we owned! All our
prized possessions, our homes, even our identity!

Nay! Look at me! Whining over these material
losses, while so many mothers from either side
have lost their sons and daughters by the thousands.
So many lost lives and relationships!
So many broken homes and families!
My people still suffer relentless annihilation
by the holocaust that continues to envelop our land.
Oh! I have seen the terror of what is war!
How I wish, I can do something to achieve peace.
I feel so sad that I now cannot do anything else
to help, except to only broadcast and write . . .

Acceptance of the unfolding destiny of the allotted
life, coupled with honest endeavour and hard work
to improve our lot, breeds contentment, which
makes coping easier, creating peace and joy . . .
I am glad that I have the satisfaction that I have
always attempted to accomplish my very best
in all what I touch in life and without surrender,
maintain the best possible relationships with everyone.

Of course, I have made several genuine mistakes.
However, I have always been true to God and to myself.
I now hold my head high with elation, as I feel
the guiding hand of God on my shoulder
and am grateful to be what I am today

59. TO A TEENAGER

Happy Birthday! Happy Birthday!
A very happy birthday to you
my eldest grand daughter, Nisha!
So you are thirteen today?
How swiftly the years have flown!
I remember it like only yesterday
when I cradled you as a crooning babe

in my arms singing all my lullabies
and telling you all the stories I know
and now suddenly cut off from apron strings
you are on the exciting threshold of life
like a fresh rose bud quivering to blossom.

Slowly the petals open one by one
to release the intoxicating fragrance within
which is its attraction! You too darling girl,
make resolve today, that you will make
efforts to continue to cultivate and nurture
unselfish love, patience and kind mannerisms
that will enhance not only your looks
but perfume your character and budding
personality too. A pretty face with good
features is only skin deep, and its beauty
will wane and fade with the fleeting years.
But a caring heart and kind gentle ways
will kindle your charisma and make
your virtue grow and glow brighter
and brighter with every passing year!
Learn to be your original natural self,
and to your own self the God within,
be always true. Let your thought,
word and deed synchronise so that

you are the same inside and outside
and you will be on the correct path in life
to be a success in all your endeavours.

60. RAMANA
1987

My darling Ramana
tall, gentle and good-natured
dimpled eldest grandson mine.
Now you are ten!
As the eldest son
you must set an example
to all the others.
Have you started to read?
Or are you still making lots
of coconut shell mud pies for fun!
You really do not know
what you are missing
when you do not enter
the magic world of books.
Start playing cricket
badminton, tennis and football.
Physical exercise will make you
healthy, tall and strong

with bulging muscles and brawn.
Just playing the piano
and army check points
will not simply do!
Be true in thought, word and deed.
Be always kind and full of care
like what you are, but improve on it
Learn to control your anger,
and also always remember
to pray and thank God
for the manifold blessings
that he has showered on you.

61. PAVITHRA
December 1988

Pretty little Pavithra
My darling little girl!
We miss your incessant chatter
and we do miss your songs and laughter.
Your dolls are still fast asleep
in the beds where you left them
I am certain that Blackie misses you
and cat Kalu misses your petting too.

Are you attempting to read?
Can you read that new story book?
Buy and read the Tamil Ambulimama.
I will always remember how you
so joyfully clapped hands
and led Sai Bhajans once
and wanted to lead more songs!
You are very musical, so learn to pick up
and sing on your own all the songs
you hear in all three languages,
Tamil, English and Sinhalese.
I am sure your pony tail would have grown.
I do hope you wear earrings at least now.
How are your art classes?
And the swimming lessons?
You must paint like an artist
and swim like a fish in 1988.
I visited your friend Anuthama
She misses her mother so much.
Please pray for her Pavithra
and pray for peace with justice too

2005
Heartiest congratulations Pavithra
You focussed, worked really hard

and have reached your goal,
2.1 in LLB (Hons) Law Degree
from Warwick University, London.
What a great achievement this is
after all the terror and trauma
of twenty years in the war zone,
evacuating Jaffna suddenly on a bicycle
as a refugee leaving everything behind,
including your beloved pet dogs, cats, rabbits,
chickens and fish! You have proved that
challenges are always true opportunities
for rapid growth and success in life.

62. RANGA
1982

Chubby cheerful Ranga!
Last of the lot
always full of smiles
with merry twinkling eyes
How I miss your singing
and early morning greeting
I will always remember
how you run around the house

refusing to wash every morning!
We have no petrol, movies or TV
We have no electricity or water still
So do think of us Jaffna folks
when you enjoy all comforts in Negombo
eating all the chocolates and ice cream!

Have you learnt to write the alphabet?
You are the last of the lot and now
you too must start music and singing.
There is a lot of music in you
That's why we all love you.

2005
How lucky you are Ranga
to be get this wonderful opportunity
to study medicine in English in Latvia.!
I wonder what specialty you will choose.
You are an exact, taller replica
of your appah, and no doubt
will gather name and fame like him.
Make maximum use of this chance
to realise your full potential
so that you can make all of us
happy and proud of you.

63. ARJUNA
1992

Darling little London Arjuna
Our latest little grandson.
First of the brood
for Kanthini and Niranjan.
Now you are six!
Not in years, but only
just six months old!
However, your budding
intelligence and individual
personality flash forth
in your wide smile
and sparkling eyes!

How exasperatingly
endearing you are
when you insist
and perform 'satyagraha'
that you simply do not
want your milk from a bottle!

May that Almighty Omnipotent
Power that is God, always

protect, help and guide you
in every endeavour and
all your varied interests in life,
to grow up to be man
of whom I can proudly say
"This is a grandson of mine."

2005
It is lovely to see that you have grown
to be so clever, handsome and tall Arjuna.
You have indeed done well to be chosen
the Head Boy in your school.
Congratulations! Keep it up!
You have become very responsible too!
I remember how you helped
me shop in London last year.

I will always remember watching Wimbledon
with you and do wish that you'll be good at tennis
too!
It is so heart-warming Arju, to watch you
with Sudha, and realize what great friends
both of you are! Keep it up and keep
up your caring, gentle mannerisms too!

64. SUDHAKAR

My sweet and smiling Sudha Kutty!
What a joy it is to listen to your British accent
which is so different to Canadian English!
Though so slender, you are full of energy
I realized this when I watched you swim
like a fish with strong strokes during your lesson.

So you are a maths and chess wizard Sudha,
winning all the prizes in a row!
You stopped the piano but like the guitar
and I hope you will learn to sing and write too!
You must follow your brother's footsteps
and become the head-boy as well
and shine as an all-rounder at school.

Childhood! Ah, it passes all too swiftly,
so touch life in as many points as possible.
Learn as many skills as you can now,
as later you will not have the time!
I feel so sorry and sad that I blundered
such a lot and did not meet you as often as I should.
have. I will definitely make amends and spend more
time hereafter with you all in London in the future.

65. ABINATH

Abi! Cherished eldest son of Ravi and Nala
The tall, fair and handsome undergraduate!
Isn't it great that some special synchronicity
in the grand kaleidoscope of the cosmos
made both of us, paternal grandma and grandson
to share the same birthday, July 13nth!
You are my best birthday present Abi,
and we do share so much in common too.

You resemble appah and your maternal grandpa
not only in looks but in your caring ways too.
You are already financially independent,
work hard for that and live at university.
Two more years will reveal the direction
your life will take. I love to watch you perform,
when you act, play the piano and sing, as music
simply courses through your young veins.
It will be so good if you decide to let it flow out
now, without denying yourself that pleasure.
Remember to continue to be genuine, watch your
words, weight, not interfere or be too demanding.
It is great that you followed Baba's Education
in Human Values, but you must also practise
all what you learnt. If you do that I am certain

188

that you will be happy and attain resounding
success in all your varied endeavours in life.

66. KANJANA
2005

I am so proud of all your accomplishments Kanji!
There is another recent feather in your cap,
with your entrance to the University of Toronto.
But you did work hard for it, didn't you?
You are keen on soccer and cross country too.
You are a confident all-rounder and it is a real treat
to hear you sing and watch you dance with such agility
with your trained voice, body language, expressive
eyes, glorious hair and white teeth forever flashing in
a smile!
You are such an attractive, 'turning heads teen-ager'.
However, I must also tell you that I can't understand
why at times you like to straighten your lovely natural
curls! Acceptance and love of yourself, siblings, family,
and your environment is the solid foundation,
so essential for self-esteem and balanced personal
growth.

You do take after Saras Grandma with your sweet tooth! I am not sure, but will you try to be a good cook like ammah?

I am sorry that I made a mistake in not teaching you Tamil.

Please make a genuine effort to learn it this summer so that you can read the words, when you sing on stage.

I have loads to teach you, but you have such tight schedules.

I like your writing and am glad that you nurture your spirit every Sunday.

However, you must practice what you learn of Human Values and cultivate gentler mannerisms to enhance your personality.

Life has been good and God has blessed you abundantly.

I am certain that you will be grand success in life.

67. GOBINATH
July 28, 1991

Gobi! My little one
My latest little grandson
God's chosen gift, the little bundle of joy
How sweet you look, with your pursed up
rose bud lips, curly hair. and enquiring eyes!
May God's choicest blessings, always surround you
with love and joy. Our Greetings to you little one
but only in spirit, as we are in Jaffna
and you are so far away in Toronto, Canada!
June 2005
You have grown tall, lean and got so tanned too
Gobi, playing in the sun! You are the leaven
in the loaf, and the house is quiet when you are out!
I felt wonderful Gobi, to watch you collect
the Principal's Award at your Graduation!
It is great that you were nominated
for English and Math and maybe
next time you will get those awards too.

I am so proud that you chose to learn Tamil
on your own at school. You say that you can
read a bit, but I am waiting to hear you talk!

Tamil is a lovely language with splended literature too.
You can teach Abi and Kanji and practice
speaking only in Tamil at home like your cousins.
I am happy that you are a voracious reader like me
and I am sure you'll be good in languages too
so, I will patiently await your first poem Gobi!

68. THE ARRIVAL OCTOBER 1997

I give thanks for this gift of our latest grandchild.
Sweet and sloe eyed, with the shock of straight hair
and limbs so long and lissom . . .

Small and fragile as you are
you have already managed to entwine
every single one of us around your
tiny little finger! Demanding constant
attention, upsetting all routine with
restless days and sleepless nights!
But you compensate all right don't you?
You do radiate so much of love and
joy, just being here . . .
What is it that you recollect so vividly
which makes you smile so sweetly
then cry in fear and run in your sleep?

I remember my grandma telling me the story!
Does that same wily fox try to frighten you too?
Whispering,"Your mother is dead?"
And you smile, "No! Ammah just fed me milk!"
But when the teasing fox continues his chase
and taunts you, "Your father is gone!"
Do you believe him and cry out in fear?
No one knows the reasons for these as yet!

When you grow up, darling Priyanka!
I wonder what career you would choose?
Why not try something on un-trod ground?
Why don't you initiate research to discover
what evokes these unexplained emotions in babies
and the reasons behind these phenomena?

2005
How quickly you have grown up Priyanka and how
lucky you are, that you are gathering so many skills!
It is a joy to hear you speak Tamil so well and with
French, you are now trilingual. You must learn to read
and write Tamil too, as the literature of our mother
tongue is as rich as the literature of other languages!
You love to read, write well, are a good dancer and
singer in both English and Tamil and you must thank

your parents for all this! However, do you know what
I like best about you Priyanka?
How good an artist you are already, and your gentle
nature!

69. PRITIKA
April 29, 2000

Welcome little Pritika!
Welcome into the fold.!
What a wonderful gift you are
to all of us around you!
You are the perfect presence
to herald the new millennium.
I am ever so grateful
to be thus abundantly blessed
again and again, with the joy
of children around me
these past five decades.

Tall, fair and long-limbed
you too like Priyanka

are as pretty as a picture.
However, you do complain
a lot more, don't you?
What shall we do Pritika
to punish that naughty wind
that plays hide and seek
within your tiny tummy?

I do find it tough to accept
some modern parenting methods.
The rules are so different now
to how I brought up my children!
Not even a sip of water
is fed to babies for six months!

2005
It is so lovely Pritika, to see you playing
and giggling such a lot with Priyanka!
Both of you are great friends and playmates!
You watch and imbibe all what Priyanka learns,
so pick up things really fast and you are
going to be excellent in every possible activity!
I will always remember, how you surprised everyone
following Priyanka on stage, when she went to collect
her singing prize! Your fractured elbow will heal
in no time and you will enjoy a wonderful summer.

70. AUTUMN

Fall has arrived once again
with that fresh cold nip in the air
as fast fading blossoms
and brightly painted foliage
all red, russet and yellow
blaze alluring autumn mellow
into my life in beloved Ontario.

I walk immersed in deep thought
to Radio Asia Canada, which bristles
with anticipation of the first ever
24-hour Tamil CRTC 1670 AM
& Astra Channel World Broadcast.

I recollect with pain and sorrow
all the losses of my beloved people,
floundering helpless unknown
and unheard by the rest of the world.
I feel so guilty that I am here
safe and sound away from the turmoil
of the unceasing warfare which still
relentlessly torments my motherland.

I didn't realise that I am still so selfish,
but honestly, I do feel relieved at last.
My displaced surgeon son in law is
transferred out of the Jaffna hospital.
My daughter's family is at last
out of the war zone. My aged mother,
sisters Chandra, Ranji and Theivika
have also joined them by ICRC ship
leaving behind all their prized
possessions. My tall and gentle
eldest grandson Ramana has joined us
here in Canada, after the trauma
of a decade of the hazards and heartaches
of the war zone and I thank God
that my immediate family
at last is safe and

71. THE MILLENNIUM
2000 AD

It's the millennium!
A brand new century!
An appropriate time
to scan my memory,
recollect the past
and evaluate my life.

Have I always been true
to God, others and myself?
Have I given of my best
in all that I have attempted?
My conscience smiles, "Yes"...
Of course I am not perfect
with my limitations and frailties!
I have made many genuine mistakes
and do feel so very sad
when I am blamed for things
I did not anticipate.

Yet, I hold my head high!
God has given me strength
perennial and I manage to cope

and have overcome lots of challenges.
I was given a new lease of life
after the nasty 1991 bus accident
when I rose with all faculties intact
after three unconscious days
from the doors of death in Colombo
with several bone fractures.
I am indeed lucky to be thus blest
with the positive attitude to accept
and make the most of all
what life has offered me.

I realize it more and more
as I grow older day by day
the validity of the eternal
karmic truth of cause and effect.
We bring with us nothing
take back nothing,
except for our deeds
and life does unfold as destined.
How else can you explain
the disparities in each and every life?

I always believed
that I was selfless

but now I am aware
how much further
I need to advance
on the pilgrim's way!
The Canadian Govt. award
plus the gold medal
from Tamil's Information*
recognizing my diverse volunteerism
over these last three decades
both in Sri Lanka and Canada
does make me feel so happy . . .

*The Canadian Tamil's Information is a free
 monthly magazine published from 1991, by
 volunteers led by Editor Thiru.S.Thiruchchelvam.

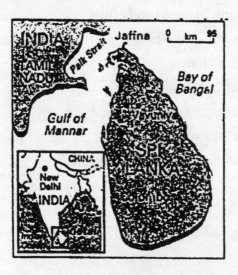

72. SITTA CHINNIAH
Psychiatrist Dr.A.Sittampalam
30. 11.1922 - 04.09.2001

Farewell! Farewell my dear Sitta Chinniah!
Fare thee well! May you rest in peace
at least now, after all your dedicated
service these last, seventy-nine years.
How true it is that the good do not suffer!
You very swiftly did step across in a flash
into the unknown, so gently and quietly like appah,
just like how you lived, without bothering anyone,
not even your beloved Puvanes, partner of fifty years,
or your precious children, grandchildren or in-laws.

Born to affluence in Ariyalai, Jaffna, Sri Lanka,
you were last of the lot, in our Viswar Arumugam
clan. You must have missed parental love, losing
them when you were tiny, but God did compensate,
didn't he? You were the pet of your siblings
and all your relations. Appah supervised your
education. You were endowed beyond measure
with intelligence and every known human
value, love, truth, patience, right conduct,
non-violence forgiveness and peace.

You climbed up and up to reach the pinnacle in
your career, both in the east and the west, but
success didn't change you. Your humility grew
more and more nobler along with it and you
were always the same inside and outside.
Your magnanimity made your Borella
and London homes, a constant 'Open House'
for each and every visitor.
You were never one to lose your temper, nor blow
your own trumpet, and no one knew that you made
history, as the first qualified Tamil Psychiatrist from
Sri Lanka. It is really great to see your name listed
in the 1995 U.K Debrets 'People of Today', but that
too was your secret, like all the other achievements
in your outstanding career and service to humanity
till the very end. But like an evil-eye, the sorrow
of losing son Yogieswaran was indeed a cruel blow,
which made you to falter and retire in March 2000.

Men may come and men may go, Sitta Chinniah,
but to find one such as you, is indeed very, very
rare. Your genuine empathy, compassion and care
has touched so many lives in so many different
ways. I am really sad that you are no more Sitta
Chinniah, but I do feel that we should not mourn

too much. We must celebrate a full and rich life
such as yours, for all what you have been and
accomplished, because many a flower is born to
blush and fade unseen, but your life will remain
a shining beacon to our future generations.

73. FAREWELL
C.T.Kanagasabapathy
1926 - 1996

Farewell! Farewell! Dear friend Kanags! Fare Thee
well! We do find it so difficult to accept how
swiftly you vanished
Stepping beyond into the unknown with such ease,
not causing any bother at all at anytime to anyone
not even to your beloved Saras or to your devoted
children. They deeply mourn and languish, unable
to bear the profound pain of the final parting, of
losing you so suddenly.
'Pasamenum pattaruthu paarickum Cheeyoney'
intones immortal Thiruvasagam. When the allotted
time arrives, our benevolent guide, The Great
Power that is God, does help and makes it easier for
us to break all our bonds and desires. God did help
you, didn't he Kanags? He ensured that all your

loved ones were away except for one. He made your departure easy, though in our ignorance we tried to hold you back hindering your last journey with our prayers. . .

It is said that what really matters in life is the quality and not the quantity. But you Kanags, were really lucky to have been blessed with both. Three score years and ten you touched, but still ramrod straight, tall, fair, handsome, confident, exuberant, outgoing and smart, always well dressed, ever ready to help anyone and everyone at anytime anywhere, with superb listening and analytical skill and advice followed by ready action. The genuine grief and sympathy of the crowd that thronged your three-day funeral from far and wide, the eulogies, garlands, flowers, gifts and messages of condolence bear eloquent testimony to your achievements and what a man you have been . . .

You lost your mother Rasammah at an early age and did not know her love and care. Your devoted father, Art Master Thambipillai nurtured you with care and concern, instilling the love of God and piety in you, which you have so successfully

bequeathed to your children and grandchildren.
You were a source of help and inspiration to your
Brothers Thamotherampillai, Ramanathan,
Ratnavel, sisters Kalaimagal and Kanthi,
neighbours, relatives, colleagues and friends.

You were blessed with the perfect partner Saras
(nee Brodie). Both of you lived for each other,
always together as a team, successfully nurturing
Indran, Kala, Nala, Keerthi, and Chandi. You
educated and moulded their lives with Mala, Jeya,
Ravi, Vanaja and Flora and fondly grand parented
Pradeepan, Gowrishankar, Praveenkumar, Mehela,
Saravankumar, Jeevan, Sudharshan, Kanjana,
Shankaran, Hindusha, Krishanthi, Jonathan, and
Johann who will all remember your love, piety and
devotion with gratitude.

You reached the pinnacle as the General Manager in
your chosen career, constructed two houses,
entertained lavishly, enjoyed every material
pleasure, not only in Sri Lanka but in
Toronto as well. You did ensure right through your
life that you nurtured spiritual growth not only in
yourself but in your family and friends too,

faithfully following your chosen path in the
footsteps of The Kaliyuga Avathar Sri Sathya Sai
Baba. You served at the Richmond Hill temple too
and dreamt of spending your final years at Puttaparthi.
But alas, in spite of your strong belief in astrology,
destiny does decide our birth and death.
The unity that binds your loved ones at this time of
loss speaks volumes about your success in life!
You had your freedom lived on your own, and did
all what you wanted to do. Well done! Well done
Kanags! Well done indeed! We wish you the very
best! May our Good Lord bless your
eternal soul to rest in peace.

21.3.1996

74. SARAS
14.9.1926 – 13.2.2000

I well remember you and your rich melodious voice
Saras, acting as the Chundikuli hero in Sakuntala.
Rather plump but attractive and fair with curly hair,
you belonged to the Christian Brodie Clan. You
realised your vocation and was teaching at prestigious

Ladies College when fate brought you and Kanags
together. Both of you were made for each other Saras
and you always complemented Kanags so well,
with your big pottu, large earrings, pleasant personality
and hearty laughter! You literally stooped to conquer!
You changed such a lot to suit Kanags, who was
a devout Hindu. He adored you, always listened
to you and as queen of your brood, you reigned
supreme!

You lived as you wished, set up home of your
own in your senior years and enjoyed every
material comfort. But life never unfolds as envisioned!
The Supreme Reaper suddenly snatched your beloved
away, before you realised what was happening!
I well remember your shock and grief as you
reeled under that cruel blow.

You changed so much Saras, after you lost Kanags.
You simply lost the will to live and wanted to join him
as soon as possible. But that's not easy, and you had
to wait for your time. Your five children and families
rallied round you, fulfilling your every wish.
Indran took you in a wheel chair to Kasi, and you
dissolved your beloved Kanags' ashes in the Ganges.

It is only when you have enjoyed every possible
material pleasure that one realises the transience of
life.
Only then can one shake off the binding bonds of
desire, to welcome the eternal joy of the life beyond.
This happened to you Saras. You must be very happy
with Kanags, wherever both of you may be now.

I feel that your life teaches a lesson
that couples should always tread the middle path,
without slanting to either extreme and should
not lean on each other too much. Each individual is
different, and all of us should pave our own unique
paths in life.
Husbands and wives must be together, but not too
close together. They should avoid stifling each other,
for the mango and the orange trees
do not grow well in each other's shadow!.

75. BRODIE HOUSE

The spacious verandah fringed Brodie House
facing the main Kandy Road, hemmed by Brodie Lane
running through Brodie lands up to Navalar Road,
was one of the first houses to be built with cement
in Jaffna. This ancient landmark which stood for
more than two hundred years, was demolished in 1986.

The well known Brodie clan, was converted into
Christianity by the early English missionaries.
A.M.Brodie, the coffee- skinned academic politician,
was a much beloved teacher at Jaffna College. Beautiful
Sinnammah, milk-skinned and sweet tempered, was
the ideal wife who dutifully catered to all his whimsical
needs.

Aunt Sobanam Gopalasingham (nee Brodie) related
great stories about how its walls were plastered with
cement and whitewashed with a mixture of lime and
egg whites for the gloss. In the earlier days, Lord
Dyke who ruled Jaffna, used to stop his horse and
have chats over the parapet wall with Gabriel Brodie.
There was a well stocked library, with a rocking chair
amidst the books. There was a special room without

windows to store the ancient coins so large in size, that money had to be shovelled with spades and tied up in sacks for transport!

Shaded by lofty mango trees, Brodie House always brimmed with entertainment and music. Every dignitary from the South visited Brodie House, including Prime Ministers Dudley Senayake, S.W.R.D.& Srimavo Bandaranayake.
No animosity or ethnic differences existed in those good old days.

A.M.Brodie proudly strutted his talented children before him and took his pretty daughters to Colombo often to perform on stage. Leela, Kamala and Saras were gifted musicians. They sang well in both English and Tamil and played the violin too. Saras especially, had a rich melodious voice and excelled in sports, while Kamala Brodie earned fame as the first Sri Lankan student of Bharatha Natyam at Kalashetra, India.
Mathurai took his family around the island for holidays to his numerous Sinhalese and Tamil friends.

The family spent most holidays at bro-in-law
Dr.Thambipillai's Pittabeddara estate and elder
brother Rajah Brodie's Rajah estate in Pittabeddars
near Deniyaya. In those days without electricity
or refrigaters, the slaughtered goat rubbed with salt
and saffron was hung up in a room to be preserved.
Dr.Thambipillai insisted that every child immediately
drink the yet warm milk that he himself milked from
his cows. Those were the good old days.

76. ARIYALAI

Our beloved hometown Ariyalai, village of our birth
in Tamil Eelam, standing as a strong stalwart sentinel
at the portals of the peninsula Jaffna, which crowns
the North of the tiny emerald isle that now is
war-ravaged Sri Lanka. Ah! I remember episodes
like yesterday, as ever-fragrant memories of our
peaceful, leisure filled life in the nineteen thirties
and forties, vivid as ever flood forth in my mind.

That first decade of my carefree childhood
cradled in my widowed granny Sinnammah's
cozy, thatched three-piece mud house, nestling

in the railway-line lane, on Ananthan Vadali Road.
I recollect how a spark from the coal mail train
lit a blaze, to burn down a house within minutes!
Like in many families, Appah worked in Colombo,
but our harmonious home was filled with love
contentment and care. As was the custom then,
we were well nurtured by Ammah's extended
family with doting uncles, aunts, helpful relatives
and neighbours. Everyone knew everybody – that
was the old Ariyalai!

We lived well, not missing any of the modern
amenities of electricity, pipe-borne water, fridge,
fan, radio, TV, etc. People drew water from their
wells with the coconut palm well-sweep, had their
own paddy fields, cows, goats and poultry too.
Everybody walked! There were very few bicycles
on the roads, but not a single girl rode the bicycle
those days! The bullock carts, Austin hiring cars
and the infrequent buses were soon outnumbered
by truckloads of soldiers, mostly African, during
The Second World War 1939 -1945.

The war Ushered in the occasional airplanes
to our empty skies. I remember the day when the

Japanese bombed Colombo only because Ammah
and all the other wives were weeping, frightened
for the lives of their husbands in Colombo.
The war brought blackouts, rations of food and fuel,
and we included wheat flour in our staple rice only
diet.
We were wary of the war, but did not suffer any
major calamities, though a few families cut L shaped
bunkers in their gardens, where we children played
house and hide and seek, along with our 'kili-thattu'
and mango seed hopscotch. That rope swing from
the mango tree for every child. Heaps of white
sand from Kilakkariyalai in every home.
The lovely scent of fresh cut mounds of golden
hay drawn home in carts, by trotting bullocks with
tinkling bells from the paddy fields, for us to
tumble in and play, before being heaped for the
year as fodder for cattle. The smell of the first
rainfall, on the thirsty ground. The fast running
flood waters we gaped at, in December.
My pets, pup Top and the kid-goat always
trailing me. The fun we had with playmates, all
the eggs, milk and curd that we enjoyed
made fresh in every home . . .

Kuttimama Thurairajah's daily ritual at dusk,
lighting kerosene lamps while the lamplighter lit
the tall oil lamp posts on the roads.
How all of us daily sat in a circle chatting after
Dinner to split the stiff fronds of fresh-cut
palmyrah 'olas' from black palms straight and tall,
so relished by our cows and goats, while listening
to lilting hit-melodies on the gramophone.
Trips in the hiring car to watch Films I recollect
like Prahaladha & Harichandra were rare treats!

I was lucky, that my skills were stimulated early
at age three, when I joined my teacher uncle
Gunaratnam to learn Tamil at Sri Parwathy
Vithyasalai, near our biggest temple of
Vara Sithy Vinayagar. This Pillaiyar Temple
and this old school, along with all the other
Ariyalai temples and schools laid the strong
foundation for spirituality, piety and the love
of our Tamil language among our youth.
It is heartening that this passion now consumes
not only me but burns bright in the hearts of
every single old boy and girl living scattered
over the globe, prompting them to send
funds to rebuild pinnacles and chariots for temples.

I recall almost every boy and girl classmate
and all the kind faces of the teachers, with the
exception of one Headmaster who believed
that sparing the rod would definitely spoil the child!

We had the usual Vani vilas, visits by school
inspectors, Health care officials and the occasional
silent film show too. Appah arranged Kamalakka
(Kamalasani Canagasingam–nee Clerical Muthiah)
to teach Chandra and me to play the violin and she
nurtured the love of Classical Carnatic music in us.
with free lessons, After grade five, I joined grade
three at Chundikuli to learn in English from 1941.
I first rode in a rickshaw, barefoot Suppan racing
with the other rickshaws! Later I walked the miles
with the others till a school bus started plying.
We shifted to our new up-stair 86 Kandy Rd.
house in 1946 and walked to College, past
the Kachcheri morning, noon and evening.
I continued my vocal and violin music lessons
under Mr & Mrs.Ananthanayagam and took part
in all the college Tamil plays like Kannaki and
The Ramayanam.

Come August and as it continues now, then too
it was festival time in all the temples in the North!
Along with Nallur, our Pillaiyar, Natchimar,
Vairavar, Uppukulam, Illanthaikulam,
Katpahavinayagar and all other Ariyalai temples
staggered their festivals so that every devotee
could worship at all the temples. In addition,
Appah, home on leave like every father,
took us out on regular temple pilgrimages.

These trips were like picnics for every family
with the breakfast chatty of kali, pittu and mangoes!
I recollect our annual, eager, early morning bullock
cart ride to bathe and worship at faraway Madduvil
temple, with the big drums, sweet pongal rice, white
brinjal curry and fried mothahams! Oh! What a
treat it was, to cross the choppy sea to adore
beloved deity Nagapooshani Amman, on the day of
her chariot festival., spend the night with our
Nainathevu island friends, and compare how lucky
we were, to live so comfortably in the mainland!

How Ammah hurried us to dress up quickly in our
long skirts, gold jewellery, a definite must then as
people would rather borrow a chain than go with a

bare neck! We wore silver/gold 'ottiyanam' for the
waist which was in fashion, and flowers in the hair,
to walk to temple with the swarming crowds, as soon
as we heard the special rhythmic beat of the temple
drum, announcing loud and clear that Sandeswarar
had started his rounds, before the poojah ritual.
We met the whole village to worship together at
these temple festivals, which were also like
carnivals to unwind, meet people, chat, shop and
enjoy the 'kathaprasangams'and nathaswarams'
and the occasional crowd drawing 'chinna-melam'
female dancers from India. There were very few
Christian families in Ariyalai then, but Catholics
from all over Jaffna flocked to the St.Anthony's
church festival at Kilakkariyalai. A Catholic church
was built on A.V.Rd. in the forties and we used
to gaze with wonder at the ceremonies! That church
is not there now though Hindus join in church worship
too.

Very few women worked those days, and many
had the same daily routine to shop for vegetables,
fish and essentials in the market-place and shops,
while the men biked to buy fish from Columbuthurai,
Pasaiyoor or Chinnakadai. Some gingelly oil and

vegetable vendors plus fishmongers walked door to door with the baskets on their head in their specified areas.

Thaipongal, New Year and Deepavali were joyfully celebrated in every home with new clothes and special sweet 'palakarams'. I recall the popular New Year Sports Meets and Fancy Dress Parades at both Kalaimagal and Pungankulam Library Community Centre grounds with nostalgia as extra special celebrations, followed by the Kalai Vila in both open air theatres. We sat on the sand and watched programs spellbound which continued till morning. I yet remember the superb portrayal of actors I.S.Shanmuganathan and Master Iyathurai in saree in lead roles in the play Manonmaniyam in the forties. Even then as now, Ariyalai folks excelled in every field. Our people adorned every sphere of life in schools and offices. Education, academics, medicine, athletics, cricket, football, Civil & Govt. Service, business, law, fine-arts, dance and song and even the parliament, with the first ever Tamil Post and Telecommunication Minister, C. Sittampalam. Our older folks are here